*Mad About*

# Mushrooms

Other books in this series:

MAD ABOUT FISH & SEAFOOD
MAD ABOUT PASTAS & CHEESE
MAD ABOUT RASPBERRIES & STRAWBERRIES

Other books by Jacqueline Hériteau:

GROW IT, COOK IT
A FEAST OF SOUPS
ORIENTAL COOKING THE FAST WOK WAY
HOW TO GROW AND CAN IT

# Mad About

# Mushrooms

## by Jacqueline Hériteau

*illustrations by Woodleigh Hubbard*

*A GD/Perigee Book*

Perigee Books
are published by
The Putnam Publishing Group
200 Madison Avenue
New York, New York 10016

Typeset by International Computaprint Corp.

**Library of Congress Cataloging in Publication Data**

Hériteau, Jacqueline.
    Mad about mushrooms.

    "A GD/Perigee book."
    Includes index.
   1. Cookery (Mushrooms) I. Title.
TX804.H47   1984     641.6'58     83-23743
ISBN 0-399-50993-3

First Perigee printing, 1984

Printed in the United States of America

1 2 3 4 5 6 7 8 9

Cover recipes include:
(front) Brandied Chicken, page 44;
(back) Sea Food Platter, page 21; Mushroom Caps stuffed with
Snail Butter, pages 32 and 33; Wild Mushrooms with Wild Rice,
page 62; Pizza with Mushrooms, page 24; Pita Broiled with
Mushrooms, page 25; Lamb Kebabs, page 30.
Flowers designed by Hunter Flowers, Park Avenue, New York City.

Copper sauté pan by Charles Lamalle, of New York City.

# CONTENTS

Food makes happiness. The MAD ABOUT books are about the fun of cooking your favorite foods—the joy of sharing new and interesting foodscapes, the satisfaction of binging—tastefully. The philosophy of the series is that when you start with ingredients that you love—mushrooms, fish, fresh herbs, vegetables, butter, eggs—and the very best recipe, you and those who dine at your table are bound to have a wonderful time. If you cook to relax as well as to eat but don't have hours a day to shop and hover over the stove, you'll truly appreciate the MAD ABOUT approach to cuisine. You will find valuable general information on the next few pages.

**Salads and finger foods 10:** from CRUDITÉES WITH BAGNA CAUDA and CRAB-STUFFED MUSHROOMS to salads, salad platters, PITA SANDWICH, and MUSHROOM PIZZA.

**Baked, broiled, flambéed 26:** from mushroom caps with steaks, fish, and on kebabs to FLAMBÉED CAPS, and caps baked with SNAIL BUTTER.

**Sautéed, creamed, puréed 34:** from CREAMED MUSHROOMS ON TOAST, and MUSHROOM PIE to omelet, quiche, soufflé, pasta, and rice dishes with mushrooms, and MUSHROOM GRAVY.

**Entrées 44:** from BRANDIED CHICKEN, STEAKS STROGANOFF, and mushroom-stuffed PORK CHOPS and SEA BASS to KIDNEYS IN CREAM, MEAT LOAF, and LAMB CHOPS.

**Exotics and wild mushrooms 58:** from CHINESE MUSHROOMS IN SHRIMP SAUCE, and MONGOLIAN HOT POT to WILD MUSHROOMS AND WILD RICE.

**Recipe list 64.**

# THE MAGIC OF MUSHROOMS

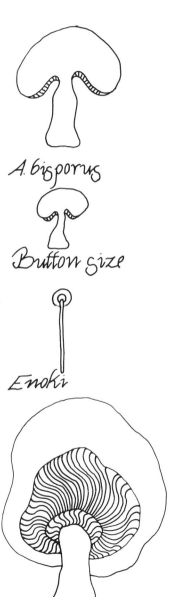

A. bisporus

Button size

Enoki

Shiitake

There is magic in mushrooms! Not the kind of magic storytellers once saw in them, inspired perhaps by the mystery of mushrooms growing in "fairy rings" (cause: blown spores), or more likely by the hallucinations some wildlings can induce in unwary mushroom pickers. No, I mean the real magic of flavor and elegance. Wild mushrooms bring a fine woodsy flavor to stews and soups and the cultivated varieties add crunch and meaty qualities to stews and salad platters.

There's more and more interest in gathering wild mushrooms. It's a rewarding focus for autumnal rambles through woods and fields and if you find a good patch of mushrooms, they are apt to return next year and can become your private garden. However, be very aware that there are deadly lookalikes to the good mushrooms. A recommended guide is Gary Lincoff's *Audubon Society Field Guide to North American Mushrooms*. In France, when my world was young on Sundays in the fall, we trooped with aunts and uncles to the pine woods by the sea to hunt for mushrooms. The village pharmacist was ready to check our haul for toadstools (the inedible ones) and keep us safe, and that was reassuring. From my French father we have learned to identify one New England field mushroom that is safe and has a woodsy taste, *Agaricus campestris*, a rangy version of the most common cultivated mushroom, *A. bisporus*. We prize firm white puffballs, too, slice and sauté them for omelets. They are edible until the color changes.

## VARIETIES TO BUY

The illustrations here are of the mushrooms we all know and love and buy, along with some of the newly cultivated and wild mushrooms beginning to appear in gourmet shops everywhere. The commercial mushrooms, top, left, are offered as big, beige-topped caps, sold loose by the pound. The buttons (under one inch) come in pressed cardboard boxes sealed in plastic. The big caps are best for baking and broiling, pages 26–27, Kebabs, page 30, and salads, pages 18–21. Buy the buttons for casseroles, and when you are in a hurry to make dishes such as Scallops and Mushrooms, page 56, and Kidneys, page 51. The recipes in this book have been tested using these mushrooms because these are the most available to everyone everywhere. The flavor is generally rather bland, so when you are cooking with flavorful wild mushrooms, or the shiitake or cèpes discussed below, reduce the quantity of mushrooms in the recipe so you won't overwhelm the dish.

The tiny enoki dake (snow puff) mushrooms illustrated here originally were grown in Japan. These are most useful as a garnish and in Oriental dishes, such as the Mongolian Hot Pot on page 60.

Shiitake mushrooms, *Lentinus edodes*, are the golden oak (East Coast) and black forest (West Coast) gourmets are mad for. They are beginning to appear fresh in markets here. They have been cultivated in Japan for 2,000 years but we used to get only dried versions sold for Chinese cooking. They are $5 to $7 a half pound in New York but production is increasing. The flavor is wild, piney, superb and a quarter pound will flavor Brandied Chicken Casserole, page 44. Similar, though less strongly flavored in my experience, are the wild cèpes and porcini, the *Boletus edulis* sought after by Italian cooks for dishes such as Chicken Cacciatore, page 50. Dried imports from France and Italy appear year round at high prices and just a few enhance stews and soups. The fresh boletes are almost as costly as the shiitake mushrooms, but worth the price!

*Morel*

Another wild mushroom from Italy is the morel, *Morchella esculenta.* It looks like a spongy little dunce's cap and appears after spring rains all over the U.S., as do its several poisonous lookalikes. Buy a few dried morels ($13. an ounce) to add pungency to mushroom-flavored soups and stews. But cook them well. Dried or fresh they can be indigestible if incompletely cooked. The beautiful golden chanterelle, *Cantharellus cibarius*, is now turning up, fresh, in specialty markets, and it is flavorful though not, in my experience, as exciting as the shiitake and cèpes  For recipes for wild mushrooms, turn to pages 62 and 63.

*Cèpes, porcini*

## HOW TO SELECT MUSHROOMS

The stem of a young, fresh mushroom is fixed to the cap firmly. As the cap ages, the stem grows out, the umbrella opens a little, and the exquisite pale-pink-beige gills (pink in the commercial *A. bisporus* and many other mushrooms) begin to darken. The flavor intensifies, too. Young mushrooms are the best buy because they will keep longer, and are firmer. Older mushrooms generally have a stronger flavor, and sometimes, in stews and soups for instance, that is good. Don't, however, buy mushrooms that are drying up or becoming dark and soggy.

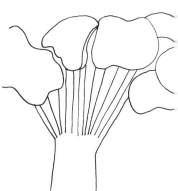

*Chanterelle*

## STORING, FREEZING, DRYING

If it happens that you buy mushrooms and can't use them at once, store them in a brown paper bag in the crisper. To keep them longer, freeze them. Just seal them in a plastic bag from which the air has been withdrawn (you can simply suck it out). Frozen, they'll keep well for a few weeks. They won't be crisp when they thaw, but they will be cookable. To have mushrooms handy for casseroles, freeze them cooked. Sauté the mushrooms with 3 tablespoons of butter per half-pound until the moisture dries, then salt and pepper lightly and freeze in a plastic container. You can include minced green onions and garlic in the cooking if you wish. They will keep, frozen, for six months at least. This is a good way to handle wild mushrooms, should you have more than you can use.

Drying is another way to keep mushrooms, especially batches of wildlings you can't use at once. Wipe them, slice a quarter inch thick, and set them to dry on clean cheesecloth on window screens in the hot sun. Or string whole mushrooms on long threads and hang in the sun. When they are totally dry—4 to 8 days, usually—store them in tightly closed paper bags in a dry closet. They are wonderful in stews and soups.

## PREPARING MUSHROOMS FOR COOKING

Even if you have purchased the cleanest caps, chances are there's a little of the growing medium sticking to them somewhere. With a clean, damp paper towel, gently wipe the caps free of sand and clinging specks. Be careful not to bruise their heads. The stems are good, though a little stringy sometimes; cut their tough ends off—but just a sliver. If the caps are dirty, wipe each one under cold running water with a paper towel and immediately wipe it dry. Clean before you stem them. Try not to get water into the gills on the underside. Mushrooms absorb water quickly.

To cut mushrooms into T shapes, leave the stems on. Turn the mushroom on its head and slice from the stem to the cap.

If you will not be using the stems in a recipe, save them for use in stews, omelets, or salads. The easy way to remove the stem is to push on it until it breaks away, leaving the cap concave and ready to stuff. If the stem doesn't break cleanly, scoop out its remains with a small spoon.

## COOKING MUSHROOMS

To sauté mushrooms, use your favorite heavy, well-seasoned skillet or any pan that distributes heat evenly so that the mushrooms will crisp well. Each recipe gives a cooking time for mushrooms. It's 5 to 6 minutes usually, depending on the thickness of the slices, but cook by eye and by nose. When the mushrooms are cooked, the moisture is almost dried up and there's a pronounced whiff of mushroominess over the stove. At that point, I have found, mushrooms have the most flavor. Sprinkle a few grains of salt and pepper over them, and allow them a few minutes to sit in their buttery coats. Cooked this way before they are put into a stew, mushrooms definitely add more flavor.

When cooking mushrooms with lemon juice, tomatoes, or other foods containing acids, try to work with an enameled or glass saucepan or a stainless-steel electric skillet. Use a slotted spoon to sauté mushrooms so you can lift them from their cooking juices and leave the juices in the skillet for further use. Two other kitchen instruments used in cooking mushrooms are a rubber spatula, for scraping up every smidgin of sauce, and a whisk. When making a cream sauce for mushrooms, stir the flour into the mushrooms and butter with a whisk; then you will have the whisk in hand when you add the hot milk, cream, bouillon, or whatever to turn the *roux* into a cream sauce. I mince mushrooms in a food processor, about a cupful at a time.

## GROWING YOUR OWN MUSHROOMS

Mushrooms develop from spawn planted in composted horse manure—manure mixed with bedding straw and composted to a rich, dark, odorless humus. You can buy spawn and growing medium in kits from garden centers. The kits can produce enough mushrooms to put you in the mushroom business. A woman I know actually did sell mushrooms grown in kits in an understair closet that was dark and cool. You must keep the mushrooms' soil moist and the mushrooms picked once they start to come in. You can also sow mushrooms in June outdoors in beds covered with composted material, as described above.

# SALADS AND FINGER FOODS

## CRUDITÉES WITH BAGNA CAUDA

**Preparation time: 30–40 minutes**　　　　　　　　　**Serves 8–10**

Heaps of raw mushrooms and crisp vegetables dipped in this hot sauce from Italy are one of the great party appetizers. I love to combine fresh mushrooms with the little fairy mushrooms called enoki-dake, or snow puff, sold here by Korean grocers. Don't rinse the mushrooms unless they really need cleaning.

| | | | | |
|---|---|---|---|---|
| 1 | pound mushrooms, wiped | | 1 | cup broccoli florets |
| 1/2 | pound spinach | | 6 | large garlic cloves, sliced |
| 2 | small summer squash | | 12 | anchovy fillets in oil, drained |
| 1 | bunch enoki or snow puff mushrooms | | 2 | sticks butter |
| 1 | cup cherry tomatoes | | 1 | cup olive oil |
| 1 | cup cauliflower florets | | | Salt and pepper |

Trim the tough ends from the mushroom stems and quarter the larger ones so all are about the same size. Pile in one corner of a large serving platter. Wash the spinach thoroughly, air-dry it, and arrange a sixth of it as a divider between the mushrooms and the next vegetables. Cut the summer squash, stemmed, into sticks, and arrange next to the mushrooms; make another spinach divider. Trim the enoki mushrooms, break into sprigs, and arrange next to the squash. Continue arranging small pieces of vegetables in groups with spinach dividers until the platter is complete. Chill.

In a small fondue dish, mash together the garlic and the anchovies. Set over low heat. Stir until the mixture thickens, then, a little at a time, stir in the butter, then the oil. Taste, and add pepper or salt if needed. Set over a fondue heating element on low, a lighted alcohol lamp, or a Sterno container, and keep warm, but not so hot the sauce continues to cook. Serve with the vegetables.

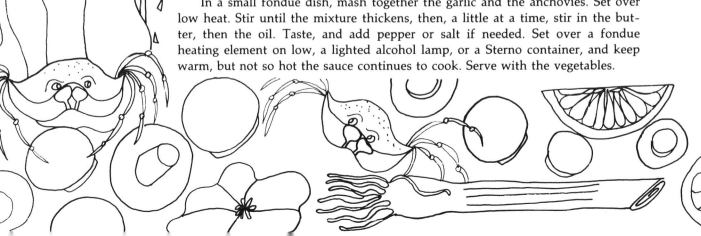

# ARTICHOKE AND MUSHROOM APPETIZER

**Preparation time: 30 minutes**
**Marinating time: 24 hours**

**Serves 10**

This serves ten as an appetizer or, arranged on a bed of escarole, serves four to six as a first course. Offer crusty French bread with it. Mushrooms selected for use in appetizers such as this one and other finger foods and salads must be creamy-white or a clear beige-pink, so fresh the stems don't dare grow out of the cap and shrivel. If you are lucky, they will be so clean you will not have to rinse them; just wipe with a paper towel.

When they are for stuffing, as here, select medium mushrooms, about 1 1/2 inches across. Buy them the day you will be using them. Keep them in a cool, dark place until you are ready to stuff them.

| | | | |
|---|---|---|---|
| 1 | pound mushrooms, wiped, stemmed | 2 | tablespoons white wine vinegar |
| 1 | eight-ounce package frozen artichoke hearts, cooked | 1 | medium garlic clove |
| | | 1 | teaspoon salt |
| 1/3 | cup good olive oil | 2 | teaspoons fresh or 1 teaspoon dried tarragon |
| 2 | tablespoons lemon juice | 1/8 | teaspoon black pepper |

Quarter the mushrooms and place stem-side up in a shallow glass bowl. Arrange the cooked artichoke hearts, halved, over the mushrooms. Place the remaining ingredients in a blender and blend at high speed for 2 minutes. In a small saucepan, over medium heat, bring this sauce to simmering. Pour at once over the mushrooms and artichoke hearts. Marinate at room temperature for 3 to 6 hours. Cover and chill overnight before serving.

**Variation: Antipasto Platter**—Mushrooms marinated as here, with or without the artichokes, are a wonderful addition to an antipasto platter (see *Mad About Pastas & Cheese*). Add garlic sausage slices, prosciutto, ripe olives, cherry tomatoes, canned, drained pimiento, and serve with hot, crusty baguettes or peasant bread and butter with the antipasto.

# CRAB-STUFFED MUSHROOM CAPS

**Preparation time: 20 minutes**                    **Serves 4**

In many recipes, you will not use the stems. Break them off by pushing them or pulling them to the side. If the stems don't part clearly from the caps, use a spoon to scoop out the cap. Before you remove the stems, cut away the tough ends of the stems and discard. Save the stems to make herb stuffing, page 46, or Mushroom Cream Bisque, page 35. These and many other mushroom recipes freeze successfully. Another nifty way to use a few mushroom stems is in an omelet, page 38. Or toss them into any soup or stew you are making, or sliver them into a salad.

| | |
|---|---|
| 1 pound medium mushrooms, wiped, stemmed | 2 teaspoons grated orange rind |
| 6–8 ounces cooked crabmeat, fresh or canned | Pepper |
| 3/4 cup mayonnaise | Tiny sprig tips basil or parsley |
| 1 teaspoon Maille mustard | 4 thin orange slices, rind on |
| 1 tablespoon lemon juice | |

Arrange the mushrooms stem-side up on a serving dish that has been covered with a lace doily or a cloth napkin. Drain the crabmeat and place it in a small bowl. Break the crabmeat apart with your fingers and discard any remaining cartilage. In a cup, combine the mayonnaise, mustard, lemon juice, and orange rind. Taste, and add more mustard or lemon juice if you wish. Stir in a generous grating of pepper. Stir the mayonnaise mixture into the crabmeat. With a small spoon, stuff the crab mixture into the caps, smoothing the stuffing with a broad knife. Press a tiny sprig of basil or parsley into each cap, and garnish the serving plate with orange slices.

# FRIED BRIE IN MUSHROOM CAPS

**Preparation time: 20 minutes**          **Serves 8–10**

Fried Brie in crispy raw caps is heaven!

| | | | |
|---|---|---|---|
| 1 | pound medium mush-rooms, wiped, stemmed | 1/4 | cup bread crumbs |
| 1 | stick butter | 1/3 | to 1/2-pound wedge Brie |
| | | 4 | basil sprigs |

Arrange the mushrooms on a doily on a serving plate near the stove. In a large heavy skillet over medium heat, melt the butter. As it froths, scatter the bread crumbs over it and fry the wedge of Brie in it, sliding and shaking the cheese so it is moving almost constantly over the hot surface, for 5 to 8 minutes. As the cheese begins to melt out the sides, quickly spoon it into the mushroom caps. Mince the basil over the caps and serve.

# CHEESE-BAKED CAPS

**Preparation time: 20–30 minutes**
**Baking time: 4–5 minutes**          **Serves 6–8**

This is a make-ahead mushroom and cheese broiled appetizer.

| | | | |
|---|---|---|---|
| 1 | pound medium mush-rooms, wiped, stemmed | 1 | cup fresh-grated Parmesan cheese |
| 1 | small onion | 1/2 | cup mayonnaise |

Set the mushrooms stem-side up in an ovenproof serving dish on a paper doily. Peel the onion and cut it into very thin slivers. Press a few slivers into the bowl of each mushroom cap. In a small bowl, combine the Parmesan cheese with the mayonnaise. With a spoon, stuff each cap, smoothing the stuffing over the top. Refrigerate until ready to broil.

Heat the broiler to high and place the dish 3 or 4 inches from the heat until the topping bubbles and turns golden brown, 4 to 5 minutes. The mushrooms will still be raw and fresh. Serve at once.

# MUSHROOMS, WATERCRESS, AND BLUE CHEESE

**Preparation time: 20–25 minutes**                    **Serves 8–10**

One of the most important things to know when you are going to feature an ingredient such as mushrooms is what flavors particularly enhance it. With mushrooms, there are a number of go-togethers, among them the blue cheeses— Danish blue, Roquefort, Gorgonzola. And watercress. The crispy stems and the peppery flavor make a good background for the creaminess of the raw caps. This recipe combines them both in an easy party appetizer.

| | | | | |
|---|---|---|---|---|
| 1 | bunch watercress | | 2 | teaspoons chopped chives |
| 1 | pound small mushrooms, wiped | | 1/2 | cup heavy cream, or more |
| 4–5 | ounces good blue cheese | | | Salt and pepper (optional) |

Wash and air-dry the watercress. Separate the branches. Pile them loosely on the side of a round serving plate. Cut off the tough ends of the mushroom stems and quarter or halve the mushrooms, depending on size. Pile them against the bed of watercress. In a blender or a food processor, beat the cheese with the chives and the cream until the mixture is as thick as whipped cream. Taste, and add more cream, chives, or salt and pepper if you wish. Turn into a dip bowl, and pass with the watercress and mushrooms.

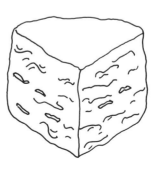

# CHEESE 'N' BRANDY RAW CAPS

**Preparation time: 20 minutes**                    **Serves 6–8**

Mushroom caps with blue cheese mellowed by cream cheese, and spiced with brandy—wonderful. The cheese-and-brandy combination, by the way, is a good spread all by itself; it tastes best ripened in the refrigerator for four days. However, it is good made at the last minute, too. The brandy here never gets cooked out, so be aware that it contains alcohol.

| | |
|---|---|
| 1 pound medium mushrooms, stemmed | 4 ounces cream cheese |
| 1 cup washed spinach, or basil sprig tips | 4 ounces Roquefort or Danish blue cheese |
| 2 tablespoons butter | 3 tablespoons brandy |
| | 1/2 cup broken walnuts |

Set the mushrooms stem-side up in a serving plate covered with a lace doily or a cloth napkin. Arrange a few spinach leaves or sprigs of basil around the edge of the plate.

In a small bowl, with electric beaters on high, whip together the butter, cheeses, and brandy to make a soft spread. With a small spoon, fill the caps and smooth the filling. Cover until ready to serve. Just before serving, press a piece of walnut into each mushroom cap.

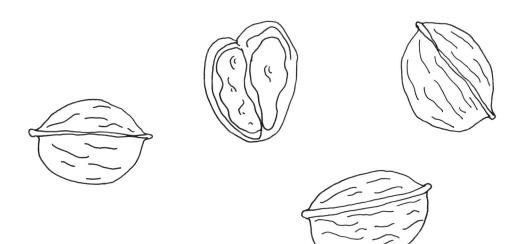

# SPINACH AND MUSHROOM TOSSED SALAD

**Preparation time: 20 minutes**
**Chilling time: 30 minutes or more**                    **Serves 6–8**

Another great combination with raw mushrooms is spinach! This is the way we make mushroom-and-spinach salad for the family. I make the salad dressing in the wooden serving bowl and slice the mushrooms directly into the dressing so they marinate before the salad is tossed.

| | |
|---|---|
| 2 small cloves garlic | 1/4 teaspoon Pommery or Maille mustard |
| 1 teaspoon salt | 8 ounces mushrooms, wiped |
| 1/8 teaspoon pepper | 1/2 pound spinach, washed |
| 1/4 cup olive oil, or more | 1/4 head iceberg lettuce |
| 1 tablespoon lemon juice | Salt and pepper |
| 1 tablespoon tarragon wine vinegar, or more | 1/2 cup croutons |
| 2 teaspoons minced or 1 teaspoon dried tarragon | 3 tablespoons butter or olive oil |

Slice the garlic into a wooden salad bowl, sprinkle the salt over it, and with the back of a wooden spoon, mash the two together to make a paste. Stir into it the pepper, oil, lemon juice, vinegar, tarragon, and mustard, and mix well. Slice the mushrooms in T shapes and add to the dressing, pile stemmed spinach leaves on top, and shred the lettuce over the spinach. Chill until ready to serve.

Toss together fifteen or twenty times. Taste and add oil, vinegar, salt and pepper if needed. Sauté the croutons in the butter or oil, sprinkle them over the top of the salad, and serve.

# SALAD PLATE WITH NUTS

**Preparation time: 15 minutes**                    **Serves 4**

This is hearty enough to make a substantial appetizer and should be followed by a light entrée, fruit for dessert, or an iced sweet. It is particularly pretty, as the mushrooms nestle like gnomes into the bed of dark green spinach. They should be small, very white mushrooms with neat stems. You may use bottled blue cheese or Roquefort dressing, but the salad will be more pleasing if you have a good homemade blue cheese dressing.

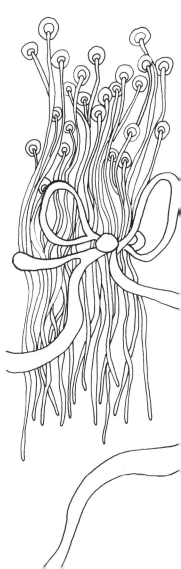

| | |
|---|---|
| 1/2  pound spinach, washed and trimmed | 1/3  cup chopped walnuts or pecans |
| 6  ounces small white mushrooms, wiped | Chunky Blue Cheese Dressing (p. 22) |

Set out four appetizer plates or small salad plates, and on each mound a fourth of the washed, trimmed spinach leaves. Divide the mushrooms into four lots and tuck these stem first into the spinach forest in a little cluster, about four or five to each plate. Sprinkle with a portion of the chopped nuts, and at one side of each plate arrange a small container (a ceramic butter pot, for instance) of Chunky Blue Cheese Dressing. Serve.

**Variation: Salad with Enoki dake Mushrooms**—Shred a quarter head of iceberg lettuce into a salad bowl, top with a half bunch of watercress, chopped; sliver a plum tomato and a quarter of a green pepper over the cress and slice 2 trimmed green onions onto all this. Sprinkle with 2 teaspoons of sesame seeds and 2 tablespoons of minced parsley, then, top with a bunch of enoki-dake mushrooms, bottom third trimmed off, broken into little groups of mushroom sprigs. Serve with Chunky Blue Cheese Dressing, page 22. This serves four.

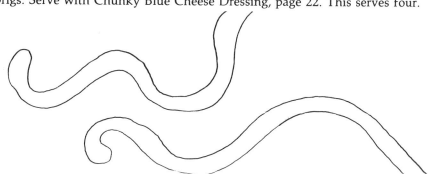

# AVOCADO AND MUSHROOM SALAD

**Preparation time: 15 minutes**                                          **Serves 4**

Select an avocado that is yielding to the touch but still a little firm. A blue cheese dressing that has chunks of cheese in it is perfect, but for a lighter dish, dress with oil and vinegar mixed with lemon or lime juice. This is rich enough to be a first course, but it also can be the salad with a meat course or roast chicken.

| | | | |
|---|---|---|---|
| 1 | head Boston or Bibb lettuce | 6 | ounces fresh mushrooms |
| 4–6 | sprigs crisped watercress | 1/4–1/2 | cup Chunky Blue Cheese Dressing (p. 22) |
| 1 | medium avocado, ripe | | |

Cut the core from the lettuce, separate the leaves and arrange around a salad bowl. Mince the watercress, including stems, into the bowl: reserve 3 sprigs. Slice the avocado in half, remove the seed, then peel the halves. Slice the meat thinly and arrange in the salad bowl. Slice the mushrooms 1/4-inch thick over the avocado slices. Pour the salad dressing over the vegetables, taking care to coat any visible portions of the avocado to prevent discoloration. Garnish with reserved watercress sprigs and chill until ready to serve.

**Variations: Mushroom Stuffed Avocado Appetizers**—Halve the avocados (you'll need one whole avocado for each two guests). Brush with salad dressing so the avocado won't discolor. Mince one sprig of watercress into each avocado half and fill with thin slices of fresh mushrooms. Ladle the salad dressing over the mushrooms, top with a sprig of watercress, and chill until ready to serve.

Or—separate the leaves of the Boston or Bibb lettuce and arrange one or two on each of four salad plates. Arrange the avocado slices on the lettuce cups and fill the cups with mushroom slices. Garnish with watercress.

# NEW POTATOES, MUSHROOMS, AND DILL

**Preparation time: 45 minutes**
**Cooling time: 1–2 hours or more**                          **Serves 4**

The salad platter on our back cover is a composite of this salad and the next two—wonderfully substantial but meatless main courses for those who prefer lighter meals. Nice with crispy, hot rolls.

| | | | |
|---|---|---|---|
| 1/3–1/2 | cup Salad Dressing Maison (p. 22) | 12 | ounces big mushrooms, wiped, quartered |
| 20 | tiny new potatoes Cold water | 1/2 | bunch leafy greens, as oakleaf or romaine |
| 1 | teaspoon salt, and more | 1 | large red pepper, seeded, cut up |
| 3 | branches fresh dill, | 6 | radishes, cleaned |
| 2 | tablespoons olive oil | 1 | recipe Mayonnaise Maison (p. 23) (optional) |
| 1 | large clove garlic | | |

Prepare the salad dressing and store in the refrigerator. Clean the potatoes (but do not peel), place them in a medium saucepan with cold water to cover, the salt and 1 sprig of dill. Cover, and over high heat, bring to a boil. Reduce the heat, and simmer until barely tender, about 20 minutes. Drain. Shake over the heat to dry and sprinkle lightly with salt. Turn into a large salad bowl and pour 1/3 cup of the dressing over the potatoes. Coarsely cut and toss the potatoes with the dressing. Taste, and add more dressing to taste if needed.

Meanwhile, heat the oil in a big, heavy skillet over medium-high heat. Mince the garlic into it and stir-fry the mushrooms in the oil and garlic 6 to 7 minutes, or until the moisture dries. Season with a tiny pinch of salt.

Arrange the greens on a salad platter and set the vegetables in groups on top of the greens. Snip dill over all and serve the platter with Mayonnaise Maison on the side, if you wish.

# TOFU AND SPRING VEGETABLES

**Preparation time: 30 minutes**                                **Serves 4**

This is satisfyingly crunchy anytime, but especially when you can find three shades of sweet pepper to make it with—red, gold, green. Remove the tough stem end before you quarter the mushrooms, and choose the freshest mushrooms you can find.

|     |                          |     |                          |
|-----|--------------------------|-----|--------------------------|
|     | Salt                     | 1   | large clove garlic       |
| 8   | ounces big mushrooms, wiped, quartered | 2 | teaspoons lemon juice |
|     |                          |     | Salt and pepper          |
| 1/2 | each of a red, gold, and green sweet pepper | 1/3 | cup Salad Dressing Maison (p. 22) |
| 1   | cup broccoli sprigs      | 1/4 | pound tofu, diced        |
| 3   | tablespoons olive oil    | 4   | green onions, trimmed    |

Sprinkle a little salt on the mushrooms and arrange them on a salad platter. Cut the peppers across the width into 2-inch strips. Prepare the broccoli sprigs, using only the green tips. In a large, heavy skillet over medium-high heat warm the oil, and mince the garlic into it. Sauté 2 minutes, then add the pepper strips, and stir-fry 1 minute. Add the broccoli sprigs and stir-fry 2 minutes more. Sprinkle with lemon juice and with a tiny pinch of salt and of pepper. Turn off the heat and arrange the semi-cooked vegetables in heaps around the mushrooms. Sprinkle Salad Dressing Maison over the vegetables and mushrooms and drop the diced tofu here and there over the platter. Mince green onions over the vegetables and mushrooms. Serve at room temperature, or chill an hour or so and serve.

# SEAFOOD PLATTER

**Preparation time: 1 hour**
**Chilling time: 1–2 hours**

**Serves 6**

An elegant hot-weather main course to serve lukewarm, or chilled. With crusty bread, cheese, a side salad of tossed greens, and sherbet for dessert, this makes a very satisfying meal. The cheesecloth wrapping makes the fish easy to handle.

| | |
|---|---|
| 8 cups water | Salt |
| 1 tablespoon salt | 1 8-ounce can water chestnuts |
| 1/2 teaspoon dried thyme | 1/2 pint cherry tomatoes |
| 1 small bay leaf | 1/3 cup Salad Dressing Maison (p. 22) |
| 1 green onion, sliced | |
| 3 1-inch halibut steaks (1 1/2–2 pounds) | 1–2 cups crisped salad greens |
| 1 pound jumbo shrimp, shelled, deveined | 1/4 small Bermuda onion |
| 1/2 pound big mushrooms, wiped, quartered | 1 recipe Green Herb Mayonnaise (p. 23) |

In a medium kettle over high heat, bring the water with the salt and the herbs to a rapid boil, covered. Wrap the halibut steaks in cheesecloth and set in the kettle. Cover, bring back to a boil, reduce the heat, and simmer 5 minutes. Add the shrimp and cook another 3 minutes. Remove the shrimp and the cheesecloth to a colander and allow to cool.

Sprinkle the mushrooms with a little salt and arrange on a salad platter. Drain the chestnuts and arrange on the platter with the tomatoes, rinsed and stemmed. Toss the shrimp in the salad dressing and arrange on the platter. Sprinkle the remaining dressing on the fish, break it into chunks, and arrange on the platter. Arrange leafy greens around the outside of the platter and sliver Bermuda onion over everything. Serve at room temperature or chilled, with Green Mayonnaise on the side.

# SALAD DRESSING MAISON

**Preparation time: 10 minutes**                    **Yield: 1 1/3 cups**

Here is a list of basic ingredients we use to make salad dressing for the family. When I have time, instead of using the blender, I slice the garlic into a wooden salad bowl, cover it with the salt, and use a round wooden spoon to mash the salt into the garlic. Then I add the other ingredients. This amount of dressing is enough for three or four salads of four portions each, made with four cups of greens, loosely packed. Makes a great marinade for mushrooms. If you have very good, fresh olive oil, use only that. If not, use half corn oil, or the oil you prefer.

| | |
|---|---|
| 1/2 cup olive oil and 1/2 cup vegetable oil | 1/2 teaspoon sugar |
| 1/3 cup Dusseaux vinegar with tarragon | 1 large clove garlic |
| 1/2 teaspoon Pommery mustard | 1/4 teaspoon dried thyme (optional) |
| 1/2–1 teaspoon salt | 1/4 teaspoon dried oregano (optional) |
| 1/4 teaspoon pepper | 4 sprigs parsley |

Combine all the ingredients in a blender or food processor, process, taste, add more of any ingredient you wish, then bottle and chill. Capped and stored in the refrigerator, this will be good for several weeks.

**Variation: Chunky Blue Cheese Dressing—**Toss 1/3 to 2/3 cup of crumbled blue cheese with the basic salad dressing after processing is complete.

# MAYONNAISE MAISON

**Preparation time: 12–20 minutes**          **Yield: sauce for 6–8 portions**

When I was about eight, my mother taught me the secret to success in making fresh mayonnaise—put a little of the vinegar into the yolks before you start beating in the oil. Add the oil almost drop by drop until the mayonnaise thickens. Added too quickly, the ingredients will curdle. If it does begin to curdle, a quick addition of a teaspoon of vinegar may smooth it out. If not, start again—yolk, salt, mustard, vinegar—and bit by bit, add the curdled mayonnaise, then complete the sauce. I can't imagine serving cold lobster, shrimp, or fish without this mayonnaise—anything else is just not quite as good! It keeps a week or so in the refrigerator, capped in a bottle, just as salad dressing keeps. Use good olive and vegetable oil, half of each.

| | |
|---|---|
| 2 large egg yolks | 3 tablespoons white wine vinegar or lemon juice |
| 1 teaspoon salt | 1 1/2 cups salad oil |
| 1 teaspoon prepared mustard, such as Pommery or Maille | |

Place the yolks into a medium bowl that narrows at the bottom so the yolks won't be scattered when you start to beat them. With a whip or an electric beater on high, beat the yolks with the salt, mustard, and 1 teaspoon of vinegar until the color begins to lighten a little. Then, almost drop by drop, add the oil. As the sauce pales and thickens, add more oil and vinegar in a very slow, very thin stream until it is all in the sauce. The mayonnaise will stand in soft peaks at this point. Chill until ready to serve.

**Variation: Green Herb Mayonnaise**—In a food processor, a blender, or by hand, mince together 1/2 cup tightly packed combination of parsley, chives, fresh tarragon, chervil, and dill. Stir into Mayonnaise Maison and chill for 1 hour. Watercress and spinach leaves may be part of the herb mixture.

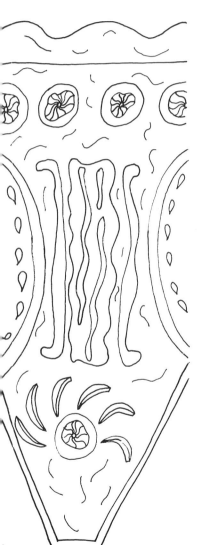

# PIZZA WITH MUSHROOMS

**Preparation and baking time: 1 hour**　　　　　　　　**Serves 4–8**

This makes dinner for four—or an appetizer for eight. Easy—and fun!

| | | | |
|---|---|---|---|
| 12 | ounces pizza pie crust mix | 8 | black olives, pitted |
| 1 | cup almost-hot water | 4 | slices thin bacon |
| | Olive oil | 1 | small ripe tomato |
| 1 | large garlic clove | 1/4 | green pepper |
| 8 | ounces mushrooms | | 14-ounce bottle pizza |
| 16 | ounces mozzarella cheese | | sauce |

Heat the oven to 425°. Rinse a large bowl with very hot water, and in it combine the pie crust mix with 1 cup of almost-hot water to make a dough. Set in a warm place and cover with a damp cloth.

Pour 2 tablespoons of oil into a large mixing bowl and crush the garlic into it. Wipe the mushrooms clean and cut the ends off flush with the caps. (Save the ends for omelets.) Cut each cap into 2 rounds and toss with the oil and garlic. On the coarse side of a hand grater, grate all the mozzarella. Quarter the olives lengthwise. Halve the bacon strips. Divide the tomato and pepper each into 8 strips.

Thoroughly oil the palms of both hands and two 12-inch pizza pie tins. Divide the dough into two balls. Pat the first ball into a flat round and set it in the center of a pizza tin. Stiffen your fingers and, with the tips, keep pressing the dough outwards, turning the tin often, until the dough covers the tin. Brush the dough all over with oil and with half the pizza sauce. Repeat the process with the second ball of dough. Bake the dough at 425° for 8 minutes. Withdraw from the oven. Sprinkle half the cheese over each crust and bake 5 minutes more. Withdraw and garnish. Place a large mushroom round in the center of each crust and arrange the other mushrooms around the outer edge of the crusts. Make spokes of the bacon, tomato and pepper strips. Arrange the black olive quarters like petals around the central mushroom rounds. Bake another 10 minutes, or until the edges are well browned. Withdraw, cool, serve in wedges.

# PITA SANDWICH

**Preparation and baking: 15 minutes**                              **Serves 1**

Pita, tomatoes and mushrooms make a wonderful little snack. This sandwich is open-faced, made right on top of the pita round. The variation below is made by stuffing the pita bread with goodies.

1   round pita bread
    Butter
2   slices mozzarella cheese
1   small ripe tomato
1   small clove garlic
2   big mushrooms, wiped, stemmed

1   teaspoon olive oil
2   tablespoons grated mozzarella
1   black olive, pitted
1   sprig basil or parsley

Heat the oven to 450°.

Generously cover the pita bread with butter on one side, and top it with the slices of cheese. Bake until the cheese melts, about 5 minutes. Withdraw from the oven. Slice the tomato into 2 or 3 rounds and set over the cheese. Crush the garlic over the tomato slices. Slice the mushrooms into T shapes and use these to garnish the tomato. Sprinkle the oil, then the grated cheese, over the mushrooms and tomato slices. Bake until the cheese bubbles. Quarter the olive lengthwise and arrange the quarters on the cheese in a circle, then center with the herb sprig. Serve.

**Variation: Stuffed Pita Sandwich**—Cut the top inch from a round of pita bread and open the pocket in the bread. Stuff into it 2 slices of bacon, halved and cooked until crisp, 2 large mushrooms caps, wiped and cut into T shapes, a thin round of Bermuda onion, 2 slices of avocado, and 1 tablespoon of alfalfa or bean sprouts. Drizzle into the opening 2 teaspoons of your favorite oil-and-vinegar dressing, and a teaspoon of finely minced parsley. Serve standing semi-upright on a bed of crisped watercress or shredded lettuce.

# BAKED, BROILED, FLAMBÉED

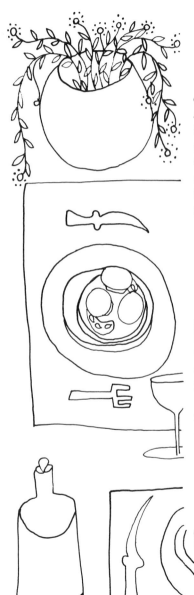

## CAPS BAKED WITH TOURNEDOS

**Preparation and cooking time: 20–25 minutes**          **Serves 4**

Mushroom caps baked with butter until they are a little shriveled have an exquisitely intense mushroom flavor, but retain a slightly crunchy texture. They are the ultimate accompaniment for an elegant steak, especially *tournedos,* beef tenderloin—filet mignon. However much it may cost, the meal will cost less than it would at a good restaurant. Add a tossed salad, an elegant Nuit-Saint-Georges red, hot crisp French bread with butter—and ummmmm! For this I choose caps 2 1/2 to 3 1/2 inches across. That is *large.* Use only very ripe tomatoes—ripened in your garden or on your windowsill. If that's not possible, garnish with cherry tomatoes.

|       |                     |       |                                 |
|-------|---------------------|-------|---------------------------------|
| 8     | large mushroom caps | 4     | one-inch-thick slices filet mignon |
| 1/2   | stick butter        | 1     | large ripe tomato               |
|       | Salt and pepper     | 1/2   | bunch watercress                |

Heat the oven to 375°.

Stem the mushrooms and wipe the caps clean. Set them, stem-side up, in a glass baking dish, and cut the butter in small pieces into the caps, reserving 3 tablespoons of butter. Salt and pepper lightly. Bake, uncovered, for 20 minutes. Check, and if the mushrooms are quite shrunken, remove from the heat; if they seem relatively raw still, allow another 5 minutes to complete the cooking. Do not spill the butter.

About 5 minutes before the mushrooms will be ready, over high heat, heat a medium-size, heavy skillet to very hot and sprinkle it with salt. Slide the filets one at a time over the skillet surface, searing them, then cook 3 minutes on the first side, reduce the heat to medium, turn, and cook another 2 minutes. Remove from the pan to a warm serving platter. Turn off the heat. Mash the reserved butter into the pan, scraping up the pan juices, and pour over the filets. Season with salt and pepper to taste. On each filet, place one thin slice of ripe tomato; top with 2 baked mushrooms. Garnish with crisped watercress sprigs, and serve.

# GRILLED STEAK WITH CAPS

**Preparation and grilling time: 30 minutes**
**Marinating time: 4 hours or more**

**Serves 6**

Here's a great steak and mushroom combination for the grill, outdoors or indoors. If you don't have fresh herbs, omit the herbs except for garlic and parsley. Serve with heaps of buttered English muffins, and a tossed salad.

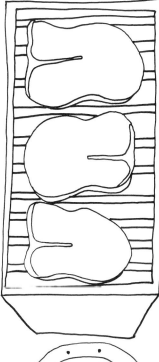

| | |
|---|---|
| 4 tablespoons olive oil | 1 large garlic clove, minced |
| 4 tablespoons minced parsley | 1 two-inch-thick sirloin |
| 1 teaspoon minced oregano, or 1/2 teaspoon dried | 1/4 cup dry red wine |
| 1 teaspoon minced basil, or 1/2 teaspoon dried | 2 tablespoons melted butter |
| 1 teaspoon minced thyme, or 1/2 teaspoon dried | 12 big mushroom caps |
| | 12 rolled anchovy fillets |
| | Parsley |

In a small saucepan over medium heat, heat the oil. Add the minced herbs and the garlic and cook 1 minute. Turn off the heat. Cut a piece of heavy-duty foil large enough to wrap the steak completely. Set the steak in the middle and bring the foil sides up close to the steak. Brush the top of the steak with the oil mixture and turn, then pour the remaining oil over the steak. Add the wine, and seal the foil. Marinate the steak at room temperature for 3 to 4 hours.

Heat an outdoor grill to very hot. Set the rack 3 inches from the heat. Drain excess wine from the foil, reseal, and set over the heat, sealed side up.

Broil the steak for 10 minutes and turn it, discarding the foil. Meanwhile, in a small saucepan, melt the butter and roll the mushroom caps in it. Set the caps near the steak and broil for 3 to 4 minutes on each side. Broil the steak for 8 to 10 minutes on the second side or until it has reached the degree of doneness preferred. Transfer to a warm platter. Set the caps on the steak and add the rolled anchovies. Garnish the platter with parsley, and serve at once.

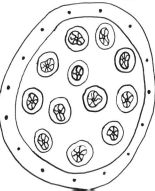

# FISH, MUSHROOM, AND HERB GRILL

**Preparation time: 20 minutes**
**Baking time: 7 minutes**                                    **Serves 4**

Another great combination—fish with mushrooms. The success of your mission will depend on the freshness of the fish. Sniff to make sure it has no fishy odor. Serve with peasant-style round bread cut into big chunks so you can sop up the juices, and a tomato salad with Brie.

|   |   |   |   |
|---|---|---|---|
| 4 | tablespoons butter | 1/4 | teaspoon salt |
| 1/2 | pound mushrooms, wiped and stemmed |  | Pepper |
|  |  | 1 1/2 | pounds bluefish fillets |
| 2 | teaspoons each minced oregano, thyme, parsley | 4 | lemon wedges |
|  |  | 4 | parsley sprigs |

In a medium-size heavy skillet over medium-high heat, melt 2 tablespoons of the butter. Slice the mushrooms thinly into the butter and sauté for 4 minutes or until the moisture bubbles away. Turn off the heat and stir 2 tablespoons more butter into the skillet. When the butter froths, stir in the herbs, and salt and a grating of pepper. At once, turn off the heat.

Cut the fillets into four portions. From heavy-duty foil, cut pieces large enough to wrap each piece of fish completely. Lay each piece of fish in the center of its foil, skin side down. With a pastry brush, brush a little of the herb butter over the skin. Turn the pieces over and spoon a fourth of the mushrooms and herb butter over each fillet. Seal the foil loosely and refrigerate until ready to cook.

Bring an outdoor grill to high heat. Set the rack 3 inches from the heat and lay the fish packages, sealed side up, on the rack. They can be touching and must be right in the center of the heat. Broil for 6 to 7 minutes without turning. Open one package and poke a knife point into the fish to check for doneness: If the fish flakes easily all the way through, it is cooked. Place one unopened fish package on each plate. Open the foil a little and set a lemon wedge in the middle of it. Add a sprig of parsley for garnish and serve at once.

# SOLE IN MUSHROOM BLANKETS

**Preparation and cooking time: 20–30 minutes**          **Serves 4**

Here's another way with mushrooms and fish. The key to success: the fish must be very fresh. Serve with new potatoes boiled *al dente* in their skins and crusted with salt, and a salad of spinach greens.

|  |  |  |  |
|---|---|---|---|
| 6 | tablespoons butter | 8 | ounces mushrooms, wiped |
| 1 1/3 | pounds sole fillets | 1 | tablespoon lemon juice |
|  | Salt | 1 | heaping teaspoon capers |
|  | Pepper | 4 | lemon wedges |

Preheat the oven to 500°.

Set a 12- or 13-inch baking dish with 3 tablespoons of the butter in it in the heating oven. When the butter has melted, withdraw the dish. Lay the fillets in the butter, then turn them over so both sides are coated with melted butter. Season with salt and pepper.

Halve the mushrooms into a food processor or a bowl and chop coarsely. Smother the fillets with chopped mushrooms, then season with salt and pepper. Bake for 15 to 18 minutes, according to the thickness of the fillets. Test for doneness: Poke a fillet with the point of a sharp knife. If it flakes easily all the way, the fillets are done. Working with metal spatulas, transfer the fillets to a warmed serving dish or dinner plates.

Scrape the pan juices into a small saucepan and set it over medium-high heat. Stir in the lemon juice and boil until reduced by half—1 or 2 minutes. Turn the heat to very low and stir in the remaining butter until the sauce thickens. Stir in 1 heaping teaspoon of capers, swirl until the frothing dies down, spoon over the fillets and serve at once. Garnish with lemon wedges.

# LAMB KEBABS

**Preparation time: 15 minutes**
**Marinating time: 4 hours or more**

**Serves 4**

Shish kebabs come from the Middle East—Turkey, in particular—where lamb is the major source of meat. This favorite kebab dish appears on our back cover. The lemon with the lamb and the rich flavor of the mushrooms suit my palate right down to the ground. I serve it with couscous when I have time to make it, or with boiled rice—or with pita or Indian bread. *Shish* means "on the skewer" and *kebab* means "broiled meat."

| | | | |
|---|---|---|---|
| 1 1/2 | pounds of boneless leg of lamb | 2 | gold or green peppers |
| 3 | tablespoons lemon juice | 1 | large Bermuda onion |
| 1/4 | teaspoon saffron threads | 18 | large mushroom caps, wiped and stemmed |
| 1/4 | teaspoon cumin | | Salt and pepper |
| 1/4 | cup olive oil | 4 | lemon wedges |
| 2–3 | ripe tomatoes | | Sprigs of parsley |

Cut the lamb into twelve pieces and place in a bowl.

In a small saucepan over medium heat, heat the lemon juice with the saffron threads and the cumin. As soon as the lemon juice boils, remove the saucepan from the heat and allow the spices to marinate for a moment or two. Add the oil, reheat to simmering, and turn off the heat. Pour the hot oil mixture over the meat pieces and toss to coat thoroughly. Cover and marinate 4 hours or overnight in the refrigerator.

Heat the broiler or the rotisserie to high.

Cut the tomatoes, seed and cut the peppers, and cut the onion, making twelve pieces of each. Thread on the four skewers, alternating with mushroom caps and meat pieces. Season with salt and pepper. Brush the remaining marinade over the skewered food, and broil 3 inches from the heat for 5 minutes on each side, or until nicely browned. Serve at once with a garnish of lemon wedges and parsley.

# MUSHROOMS FLAMBÉED

**Preparation and baking time: 35 minutes**        **Serves 4**

For me, there's no more gala first course than a flaming platter of mushrooms. Here is a fabulous starter for an elegant meal, as easy as it is dramatic. Follow with a grilled meat or fish and a tossed salad. Serve peasant-style bread chunks with the mushrooms—or you'll weep over wasted gravy!

| | | | |
|---|---|---|---|
| 12 | large mushrooms, wiped | 1/4 | teaspoon salt |
| 1 | large clove garlic | 1/8 | teaspoon pepper |
| 1/3 | cup heavy cream | 2 | tablespoons brandy |
| 3 | tablespoons butter | | |

Heat the oven to 350°.

Remove the tough end of the mushroom stems and break the stems from the caps. In a food processor or by hand, chop the stems with the garlic. Set the caps stem-side up in an oven-proof shallow baking dish that is suitable for serving and press a little of the stem-garlic mixture into each cap. In a small saucepan over medium heat, bring the cream, butter, salt, and pepper, to a simmer and spoon over the caps.

Bake the caps for 20 minutes, withdraw from the oven and carry to the dining table. Pour the brandy into a small, long-handled ladle, heat thoroughly over a stove burner in the kitchen or over a Sterno or candle flame at the dining table. Tilt the heated brandy toward the flame until it lights, and pour at once over the hot mushrooms. Spoon the flaming sauce over the mushrooms as long as the flames last. Serve.

# CAPS BAKED WITH SNAIL BUTTER

**Preparation and baking time: 30–40 minutes**  **Serves 6–8**

These mushroom caps baked with their aromatic fresh herb stuffing often elicit real groans of pleasure! To serve as appetizers, choose small to medium very crisp and fresh caps, between 1 and 1 1/2 inches across. To serve the stuffed caps as part of an hors d'oeuvres plate or as a "starter," choose larger caps and cook for another 4 or 5 minutes.

| | |
|---|---|
| 1 recipe Snail Butter (p. 33) | 1 small bunch watercress |
| 1 pound small mushrooms, wiped and stemmed | |

Heat the oven to 375°. Prepare the Snail Butter.

Turn the caps stem-side up and smooth a little Snail Butter into the bowl of each cap, then set in a glass baking dish. Bake for 20 minutes and check: If the caps are still raw-looking, cook for another 5 minutes. Arrange the mushrooms on a plate covered with a doily, and garnish with watercress.

# SNAIL BUTTER

**Preparation time: 10 minutes**                    Yield: 1/2 cup

Think of the aroma when the waiter is bringing your order of broiled snails to the table: Snail Butter it is! This butter draws strong men to the kitchen to kiss the cook and turns almost any grilled meat or fish into a dish fit for a king. It's absolutely great as a mushroom stuffing and nifty for making garlic bread. (See *Mad About Pastas & Cheese*.) The quantity here will stuff up to a pound of mushrooms, depending on the size and shape—some are more hollow than others. Be sure to broil the mushrooms until they are cooked; it takes an extra 5 to 10 minutes, in my experience, when the caps are stuffed. The mixture stays fresh in the refrigerator for 10 days to 2 weeks.

| | | | |
|---|---|---|---|
| 1 | small bunch parsley | 3 | large garlic cloves |
| 2 | big green onions | 1 | stick soft butter |

Rinse, stem, and air-dry the parsley. In a food processor or a blender or in a bowl by hand, mince the parsley until it is really fine. Turn into a saucer, then measure 2 heaping packed tablespoons back into the processing bowl. Trim away 2 or 3 inches from the tops of the onions, peel off the outer skin, mince the onions and the garlic, and mix with the parsley until it is as fine as possible. Beat the butter into the herbs until well combined. The butter will be a beautiful pale green. Scrape into a small container that has a lid.

Use as needed, and store in the refrigerator.

# SAUTÉED, CREAMED, PURÉED

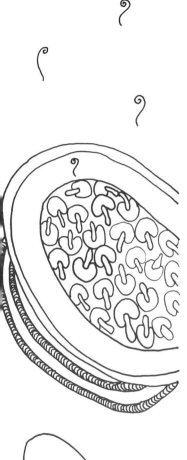

## CREAMED MUSHROOMS ON TOAST

**Preparation time: 15 minutes**                               **Serves 4**

In the recipes in this section, it is important to know when the mushrooms are done. When sautéing mushrooms—most of the dishes begin that way—you will see that there is a point about 2 or 3 minutes into the cooking when the mushrooms have given off a lot of moisture. This is an in-between stage, and if you take the mushrooms off then, they will be limp and rather tasteless. But if you sauté the mushrooms for another 2 to 4 minutes, the moisture will dry and the mushroom flavor, magically, will be stronger than when the mushrooms were raw. At this moment add just a pinch of salt, a grating of fresh black pepper, and the mushrooms are heavenly! For the recipes in this section, the mushrooms need not be ultra fresh, sublimely velvety, or untouched. More mature mushrooms have more flavor. This recipe makes a nifty brunch or a great midnight supper with a little salad and champagne. It also is a good side dish for grilled meat courses.

| | | | |
|---|---|---|---|
| 1/2 | cup butter | 1 | tablespoon all-purpose flour |
| 1 | pound small mushrooms, wiped and stemmed | 1/2–2/3 | cup heavy cream Nutmeg |
| 3 | large cloves garlic Salt and pepper | 4 | slices good toasting bread |
| 1 | teaspoon grated lemon rind | 2 | teaspoons minced parsley |

In a large heavy skillet over medium-high heat, melt the butter, and in it sauté the mushrooms for 2 or 3 minutes, shaking the pan often. Mince the garlic, sprinkle over the mushrooms, and stir and cook until the moisture dries, about 2 to 4 minutes more.

Turn off the heat, salt the mushrooms very lightly, add a grating of fresh pepper, and stir in the grated lemon rind. Reduce the heat to low. Return the skillet to the heat and stir in the flour, scraping up the pan juices. Pour in 1/2 cup of the cream, and with a whisk, stir and cook until the sauce thickens. Add a pinch of nutmeg. If the sauce is too thick, add a little more cream. Turn off the heat. Taste, and add salt and pepper if desired.

Toast the bread and remove the crusts. Cut the toast into diagonals, and on small salad plates, arrange the diagonals facing each other. Scrape a quarter of the mushrooms and cream over each piece of toast, garnish with a dusting of parsley, and serve at once.

## MUSHROOM CREAM BISQUE

**Preparation and cooking time: 25 minutes**          **Serves 4**

This is the world's freshest, yummiest mushroom soup. It is made (of all things) with clam juice from a bottle. I use Doxee Clam Juice and very clean white mushrooms packed in cellophane.

| | |
|---|---|
| 8 ounces clean mushrooms | 3 eight-ounce bottles clam juice |
| 3 tablespoons butter | |
| 1/2 teaspoon salt | 1 cup heavy cream |
| 1/8 teaspoon pepper | 1 teaspoon minced parsley |
| 3 tablespoons all-purpose flour | |

In a food processor, a blender, or by hand, chop the mushrooms coarsely. In a large heavy saucepan over medium heat, sauté the mushrooms in the butter, stirring, for about 4 minutes. Season with salt and pepper. Turn the heat to low and stir in the flour until it makes a gummy roll. Cook for another 2 minutes, then, beating constantly, stir in the clam juice. When the bisque smooths out, cover and simmer for 10 minutes more. Stir in the cream, and turn off the heat. Serve garnished with minced parsley.

# MUSHROOM PIE DIANA

**Preparation time: 30 minutes**
**Baking time: 35 minutes**                                    **Serves 8**

This thick-crusted pie with its hint of sherry is delicious as a side dish with grilled meats and makes an elegant main course for lunch. Add a spinach or watercress salad and a glass of chilled rosé, if you wish.

|     |                          |     |                        |
|-----|--------------------------|-----|------------------------|
| 1   | pound large mushrooms, washed | 1/4 | cup all-purpose flour |
| 1/2 | stick butter             | 1   | cup hot beef bouillon  |
| 5   | green onions, trimmed    | 1   | cup heavy cream        |
| 1   | large clove garlic       | 1/4 | cup dry sherry         |
| 1   | teaspoon salt            |     | Dough for a 2-crust pie |
|     | Fresh black pepper       |     | Milk                   |

Heat the oven to 375°.

Remove a thin slice from each mushroom stem. In a large, heavy skillet over medium-low heat, melt the butter. Mince the onions and garlic into the butter. Quarter the mushrooms and cut them into pieces the size of a small mushroom, dropping them into the skillet as you work. Stir in salt, pepper, flour. Working quickly, stir the bouillon and cream at once into the mushrooms, and stir until the sauce is smooth. Add sherry and cook for another 5 minutes. Add more salt and pepper if desired. Turn into a round Pyrex or enamel dish 2 inches deep and 9 inches around or a dish 10 by 7 or 8 inches.

Roll out all the dough to make a thick crust that fits over the dish. Fix the crust edges over the sides of the dish, prick the crust to vent the steam, and brush lightly with milk to help it color. Bake for 35 minutes, or until crust is golden brown.

# SHRIMP-STUFFED PATTY SHELLS

**Preparation time: 30–40 minutes**                                **Serves 8**

Patty shells are made of puff pastry. Some bakers refer to them as *vol-au-vent* (large) and *bouchées* (small). This recipe fills eight large main-course shells or twelve to fourteen small hors d'oeuvres shells.

| | |
|---|---|
| 8 large frozen patty shells | 12 ounces mushrooms, wiped |
| 20 ounces bottled clam juice (2 1/2 cups) | Salt, pepper, nutmeg |
| 1 small bay leaf | 3 tablespoons all-purpose flour |
| 1/4 teaspoon dried thyme | 1 tablespoon lemon juice |
| 1 pound small, shelled, deveined shrimp | 1/2 cup heavy cream, and more |
| 4 tablespoons butter | 1 tablespoon minced parsley |

Bake the patty shells following package instructions; scoop out and discard the uncooked dough in the center.

In a small saucepan over medium heat, bring the clam juice, with the bay leaf and thyme, to a rapid boil, and turn the shrimp into it. Cover, bring back to a simmer, reduce the heat, and cook covered for 3 minutes. Lift the shrimp from the broth, and reserve the liquid. Discard the bay leaf.

In a medium-size heavy skillet over medium-high heat, melt the butter and slice into it the mushrooms. Stir and cook for 5 to 6 minutes, or until the moisture has disappeared. Season with salt, pepper, and nutmeg. Remove from the heat, and stir in the flour. Turn the heat to low. Pour the hot shrimp water over the paste in the skillet, and stir quickly until the sauce smooths and thickens. Return the skillet to the heat. Stir and cook until the sauce is thick. Stir in the lemon juice and heavy cream. Mix in the shrimp, and more cream if needed. Divide among the patty shells. Cover with the patty shell top, dust with parsley, and serve.

# OMELET FOR ONE

**Preparation and cooking time: 10–15 minutes**                    **Serves 1**

Mushrooms and eggs are a beautiful duet! But it pays to sauté the mushrooms first in butter—lots more flavor. An omelet is the easiest of the mushroom-egg dishes to make. It's an ideal way to use up leftover plump, fresh mushroom stems.

|         |                              |     |                          |
|---------|------------------------------|-----|--------------------------|
| 4       | tablespoons butter           |     | Pinch of pepper          |
| 1       | green onion, trimmed          | 2   | large eggs               |
| 1/3–1/2 | cup sliced raw mushrooms      | 1   | tablespoon water         |
| 2       | sprigs each parsley,          | 1   | teaspoon Pommery or      |
|         | oregano, thyme                |     | Maille mustard           |
|         | Pinch of salt                 |     | Oil                      |

In a small skillet over medium heat, melt 2 tablespoons of the butter, mince the onion into it, add the mushrooms and stir and cook for 5 or 6 minutes or until moisture disappears. Mince in the herbs and cook for 1 minute more. Season with salt and pepper, and remove from heat.

While the mushrooms are cooking, with a whisk beat the eggs, water and mustard until the eggs are frothy—about thirty to forty turns of the whisk. Place an omelet pan or a pancake skillet over medium heat, wipe it with a scrap of paper towel moistened with vegetable oil, melt 1 tablespoon of butter in the pan, and heat for 2 or 3 minutes. Turn the eggs into the pan and when they begin to set, sprinkle the mushroom mixture over half the omelet. When the eggs are set but still moist on top, slide a metal spatula under the edge that has no mushrooms, lift it, and turn it over the mushroomed half so the edges fit perfectly. If the eggs are still moist, the edges will seal and the omelet will puff up as it cooks for 2 minutes more. Top with the remaining butter. Serve at once.

# QUICHE AUX CHAMPIGNONS

**Preparation and baking time: 1 hour**                    **Serves 8**

The perfect brunch when you love the guests. Make your own favorite pie dough from scratch—or be lazy and buy a shell. The rest is easy; just don't underbeat the eggs!

| | | | |
|---|---|---|---|
| 1 | nine-inch pie shell | 1 | tablespoon all-purpose |
| 8 | slices thin bacon | | flour |
| 4 | eggs | 1 3/4 | cups half-and-half |
| 8 | ounces mushrooms, wiped | 1/2 | teaspoon salt |
| 2 | green onions, trimmed | 1/8 | teaspoon pepper |
| 3 | tablespoons butter | | Pinch of nutmeg |
| 1 | teaspoon grated lemon | | Butter |
| | rind | | |

Bake the pie shell, and set the oven at 375°. Sauté the bacon until crisp, and drain on paper towel. Break the eggs into a large bowl and brush the shell bottom and sides with a little white from the eggs.

Slice the mushrooms thin, and mince the onion. In a medium-size skillet over medium-high heat, melt the butter, and in it sauté the mushrooms and onions 5 or 6 minutes, or until the moisture dries. Remove from the heat and turn the heat to low. Sprinkle mushroom mixture with lemon rind and flour, and stir to make a smooth paste. Return the skillet to the heat. All at once, pour the half-and-half over the mushrooms and stir quickly until a smooth sauce forms. Simmer, stirring, for a minute or two, and turn off the heat.

Beat the eggs with an electric beater until thick and lemon-colored. Season with salt, pepper, and nutmeg, then beat in the mushroom sauce. Crumble the bacon into the pie shell. Scrape the egg mixture into the pie shell. With a hand grater, grate a tablespoon or two of cold butter over the top of the quiche, and bake for 30 to 35 minutes or until a knife inserted into the center of the custard comes out clean. Serve at once or the quiche will fall, as a soufflé does.

# MUSHROOM SOUFFLÉ

**Preparation and baking time: 1 1/4 hours**                    **Serves 4**

I am mad about the specialness of a soufflé—the mystique of its rising, the cliff-hanging suspense of its potential, and alas, inevitable, fall. To minimize the latter, I own soufflé dishes in the right size—1 and 2 quarts. And I always beat the eggs to a fare-thee-well (lots). And I rush the soufflé to the dinner table shouting for attention as I go!

| | |
|---|---|
| 5 large eggs | 1/2 cup milk |
| 3 tablespoons butter | 1/4 teaspoon cream of tartar |
| 4 green onions, trimmed | Pinch of salt |
| 8 ounces mushrooms, wiped | 4 tablespoons butter (for |
| 1/4 teaspoon salt | soufflé mold) |
| 3 tablespoons all-purpose flour | 1 tablespoon minced chives or parsley |
| 1/4 cup sherry | |

Heat the oven to 400°. Put the eggs in a large bowl filled with warm water.

In a medium-size heavy skillet over medium-high heat, melt the butter. Slice the onions and the mushrooms into it. Sauté until the moisture starts to go, 5 or 6 minutes, and season with salt. Take the skillet from the heat and stir in the flour to make a smooth paste. Return to low heat and stir in the sherry and the milk. Beat quickly until a smooth sauce forms, and cook for another minute or so. Turn off the heat.

Drain and dry the eggs. Separate the whites into the warmed bowl and the yolks into the mushroom mixture. Immediately beat the yolks into the mushroom mixture and scrape into a large bowl. Beat the whites with the cream of tartar and a pinch of salt until they form dry peaks. With a whisk, gently stir a third of the whites into the mushroom mixture, then stir in the rest of the whites, combining completely but mixing very gently.

Butter a 2-quart soufflé mold generously and scrape the mixture into it. Bake for 45 minutes without opening the oven. Serve at once, sprinkled with a green herb.

# GREEN BEANS WITH MUSHROOMS

**Preparation time: 20–25 minutes**                    **Serves 4**

For this to be magnificent, you need very young, slender green beans from your own (or anyone's) garden. The greengrocers here sometimes have this delicacy, and I grab the beans whatever the price. They may be a little limp from having been picked awhile ago, but they perk up when rinsed in cold water and crisped for a few hours. For this dish, I choose brown-beige mushrooms, the kind that are sold loose by the pound.

| | | | |
|---|---|---|---|
| 3–4 | quarts water | 1/2 | pound medium mushrooms, wiped |
| 1 | tablespoon salt | | |
| 1/2–2/3 | pound tender green beans | | Salt and pepper |
| 2–3 | branches fresh dill | 1/4 | cup heavy cream |
| 1/2 | stick butter | 1 | tablespoon butter |
| | | 2 | tablespoons sliced almonds |

In a large covered kettle, over high heat, bring the water with the salt to a rapid boil. Meanwhile, snip the ends from the beans. Uncover the water and toss in the beans a few at a time without letting the water stop boiling. Add the dill and cook the beans, uncovered, until just tender: Take them off before the dark green turns yellow-green. Drain and return to the kettle to dry over the heat. Discard the dill.

While the beans are cooking, in a large skillet over high heat, melt the butter. Slice the mushrooms into it in thin slices. Stir and fry for 5 or 6 minutes—until the mushrooms are well dried—then season with a few grains of salt and pepper and remove from the heat. Turn the beans into a warmed serving bowl and scrape the mushrooms over the beans. Pour the cream over the beans and toss together. Return the skillet to the heat. Melt the 1 tablespoon of butter in the skillet. Sauté the almond slices in the butter just long enough to color them golden, and scrape them out over the beans and mushrooms. Serve hot.

# TORTIGLIONI WITH MUSHROOMS

**Preparation time: 30 minutes**      **Serves 4**

Tortiglioni are the twisty noodles. We love this with chicken legs roasted on the broiler, and it is great with chicken livers sautéed in butter and a little sherry. This is just as good, if not so pretty, made with other forms of pasta, such as shells and noodles.

| | | | |
|---|---|---|---|
| 1 | stick of butter | 1 | teaspoon minced oregano |
| 1 | bunch green onions, trimmed | 4–5 | quarts water |
| 1 | large garlic clove | 2 | tablespoons salt |
| 12 | ounces mushrooms, wiped | 1/2 | pound tortiglioni |
| 2 | tablespoons minced parsley | 1/4 | cup fresh-grated Parmesan cheese |
| 1 | teaspoon minced thyme | | Salt and pepper |

In a big, heavy skillet over medium heat, melt the butter, and mince the onions and the garlic into it. Sauté for 2 minutes. Add the mushrooms and sauté for 6 minutes. Stir in the parsley, thyme, and oregano, cook a minute more and turn off the heat.

Meanwhile, in a big, covered kettle over high heat, bring the water with the salt to a rapid boil, and in it cook the tortiglioni until just tender. Drain. Turn the tortiglioni into the skillet and toss with the mushrooms, herbs, and butter two or three times, then sprinkle the cheese over the pasta and toss many times, until the cheese has melted. Taste and add salt and pepper to suit yourself, then serve.

# RICE WITH MUSHROOMS AND GARLIC

**Preparation time: 10 minutes**                                    **Serves 4**

This is the easiest thing in the world and makes a heavenly alternative to ordinary boiled white rice. Great with hamburgers. You can give the same treatment to cooked noodles. I am mad about it! It's a great way to use mushroom stems left over from a dish calling for caps alone. Start the mushrooms as the rice finishes cooking. It takes minutes.

| | | | |
|---|---|---|---|
| 1/2 | stick butter | 1/4 | cup minced parsley |
| 3 | large cloves garlic | 4 | cups cooked white rice |
| 1 | cup sliced mushrooms | | |

In a big saucepan over medium heat, melt half the butter until it froths, and mince the garlic into it. Stir the garlic around, then stir in the mushrooms and cook for 5 or 6 minutes, or until the moisture dries. Stir in the remaining half of the butter, and as it froths, stir in the parsley. Cook for 30 seconds to 1 minute, then scrape over the rice. Toss together for a few moments, then turn the rice into the skillet to get up all the pan juices. Serve hot.

**Variation: Pan Gravy with Mushrooms**—Follow the basic procedure above to make a rich mushroom gravy for pan-fried steaks and chops. (The gravy will be richest if you sauté in a big, well-seasoned, cast-iron skillet.) When the meat is cooked, keep it warm, and return the pan to the heat on medium. Mince into the fat and drippings in the pan a small clove of garlic. Slice fresh, clean mushrooms into the skillet. Make the slices about 1/8 inch thick and allow 4 or 5 medium mushrooms per meat portion. Stir and fry until the mushrooms begin to render their moisture, and at once remove the pan from the heat. Stir in a tablespoon or two of bouillon, soup stock, or water, scraping up and dissolving the caramelized drippings sticking to the bottom of the pan. The drippings are the source of the intense flavor in good gravy. If the gravy is thin, stir in a little butter. Heat briefly, season with salt and pepper to taste, and serve over the meat.

# ENTRÉES

## BRANDIED CHICKEN

**Preparation and cooking time: 35–45 minutes**          Serves 8–10

Mushrooms dress dishes in a way that makes what might have been a mere stew into an elegant casserole or *blanquette* ("creamed casserole"). This is the recipe shown on the front cover. Heaven made with 1/4 pound fresh, wild cèpes.

| | | | |
|---|---|---|---|
| 3 | large chicken breasts, boned, divided (3–4 pounds) | 1 | pound large mushrooms, wiped and quartered |
| 1 | teaspoon salt | 1/4 | teaspoon salt |
| 1/4 | teaspoon pepper | 2 | green onions, minced |
| 1/4 | teaspoon curry powder | 2 | tablespoons brandy |
| 1 | tablespoon olive oil | 1 | cup crème fraîche or heavy cream |
| 4 | tablespoons butter | 2 | teaspoons cornstarch |
| 1 | large garlic clove | 1/2 | cup clam broth |
| | | | Salt and pepper |

Rinse and wipe the chicken pieces, and rub them all over with the salt, pepper, and curry powder. In a large, heavy skillet over medium heat, warm the oil and melt 2 tablespoons of butter in it, and sauté the chicken pieces until golden brown on both sides, about 10 to 15 minutes. Turn the heat to low.

Meanwhile, in another large skillet over medium-high heat, melt the remaining butter. Mince the garlic into it. Sauté the quartered mushrooms in the butter for 5 or 6 minutes or until the moisture dries. Salt them, toss the onions with them and scrape the mixture into the chicken skillet. Continue to cook the chicken until it has cooked a *total* of about 15 to 20 minutes.

In a small ladle with a long handle, over a gas burner or a candle, heat the brandy until the edges bubble a little, then, tilt the brandy toward the flame until it ignites. Pour over the chicken, shaking and tilting the pan with your hand to spread the flames around. Then spoon the flames over the chicken for as long as they are burning. Mix the cream and the cornstarch into the broth, then stir the broth into the pan, scraping up the pan juices. Tilt the pan so all the sauce flows to one side and stir this as it cooks and thickens—about 5 minutes. Season with salt and pepper. Spoon over the chicken, turn into a serving dish and serve.

# CHICKEN AND WINE CASSEROLE

**Preparation time: 10 minutes**
**Cooking time: 1 hour 10 minutes**

**Serves 6**

Here we go mushrooming a whole chicken dressed in a little dry white wine. If you don't have a bottle of wine around your house to borrow a cupful from, you will probably find special "cooking wine" that is salted in the local gourmet shops. It's not my first choice for cooking, but it's fine. My son David calls this the company chicken.

| | |
|---|---|
| 3 1/2 pound whole chicken | 1 small bay leaf, crumbled |
| 1 teaspoon salt | 1 teaspoon dried thyme |
| Pinch of pepper | 1/2 cup dry white wine |
| 3 tablespoons butter | 1 cup chicken bouillon |
| 2 bunches green onions, trimmed | 2 tablespoons minced fresh parsley |
| 1/2 pound washed mushrooms, sliced thin | |

Freeze the giblets and liver for another time. Tuck the chicken wing tips behind its back; turn it over. Slice the chicken down its back, cutting through the ribs. Turn it onto its back and flatten the breast. Salt and pepper it.

In a 14-inch cast-iron skillet, over low heat, melt the butter. Press the chicken breast-down into the skillet, and set a weight on it to keep it flat. (I use a plate and a kettle full of water.) Cook over medium-low heat for 25 minutes. Remove the weight. Slice the onions into pieces 1/4 inch long over the chicken, add the mushrooms, the bay leaf, the thyme, the wine, half the bouillon, and the parsley. Put the weight on again, raise the heat a little, and cook 45 minutes longer. Add more bouillon as the juices dry out. Set the chicken and the mushrooms onto a serving platter. Pour a little more bouillon into the skillet, and scrape up the pan juices. Cook until the gravy thickens a little, and serve over the chicken and mushrooms.

# MUSHROOM STUFFING WITH HERBS

**Preparation time: 12 minutes**

What makes the best stuffing in the world? Mushrooms! This is a version of the famous Duxelles. Half this amount will stuff a pound of mushrooms, four chops or fish fillets, twenty-four clams, twelve shrimp. The whole of it will stuff a 3- to 6-pound whole fish. It is so good you'll be tempted to eat it all by itself! Marvelous grilled or baked in the recipes on page 47.

| | | | |
|---|---|---|---|
| 6 | tablespoons butter (2/3 stick) | 1/8 | teaspoon pepper |
| 1/2 | medium onion | 1/2 | cup heavy cream |
| 8 | ounces mushrooms, wiped | 8 | double or 16 single saltine crackers, reduced to crumbs |
| 1 | large clove garlic | | |
| 1 | small bay leaf | 2 | tablespoons minced parsley |
| 1/2 | teaspoon dried thyme | | |
| 1/2 | teaspoon dried tarragon | 3 | tablespoons fresh-grated Parmesan cheese (optional) |
| 1/4 | teaspoon salt | | |

Set a large, heavy saucepan over medium heat and melt the butter in it. Meanwhile, in a food processor, a blender, or by hand, mince the onion and mushrooms. Mince the garlic, add to the hot butter, stir in the onion and mushroom mixture with the bay leaf, crumbled, and the thyme, tarragon, salt, and pepper. Reduce the heat to low. Stir and cook for about 7 minutes or until the moisture is drying out. Stir in the cream and simmer for 3 to 4 minutes, then stir in the crackers and cook 1 minute more. Stir in the parsley and cook 1 minute more. Remove from the heat.

Press lightly over whatever ingredient you are stuffing, and sprinkle with grated Parmesan cheese if the dish is to be cooked under a broiler.

# MUSHROOMS STUFFED WITH MUSHROOMS

**Preparation and broiling time: 30 minutes**                    **Serves 4**

The recipes that follow are some of the dishes you can prepare with Mushroom Stuffing Duxelles style, page 46.

| | |
|---|---|
| 12 large mushroom caps, wiped and stemmed | 1/3–1/2 recipe Mushroom Stuffing with Herbs (p. 46) |

Heat the broiler to high.

Set the mushrooms stem-side up in a glass baking dish and fill with Mushroom Stuffing; don't pack it down. Sprinkle with grated Parmesan cheese and broil 3 inches from the heat for 10 minutes, or until the cheese colors. Serve at once.

**Variations: Sea Bass Stuffed with Mushrooms**—Set a 3- to 4-pound whole sea bass, very fresh, in a 30-inch-long sheet of heavy-duty foil. Rub all over with good olive oil and stuff the cavity with Mushroom Stuffing. Bake 30 minutes at 400°. Open the foil, pour 1/2 cup bottled clam juice over the fish, close the foil, and bake for 30 minutes more. Turn the cooking juices into a small saucepan and boil down to reduce by half. Stir in 1/2 stick of butter, pour over the stuffed baked fish, and serve. Serves 4.

**Fish Fillets Stuffed with Mushrooms**—To serve four to six people, buy 4 thin, large fillets of flounder, sole, or other white fish. Salt and pepper each side, and set 2 of the fillets in a baking dish smeared with 3 tablespoons of soft butter. Cover each fillet with 1/2 recipe Mushroom Stuffing; cover with the reserved fillets. Pour 1/4 cup bottled clam juice over the fillets, dot with butter, and bake at 400° for 15 to 20 minutes. Serve with lemon wedges and parsley as garnish.

**Shrimp Stuffed with Mushrooms**—To serve four people, peel, devein and rinse 12 jumbo shrimp, but don't remove the tails. Cut partially through each tail, press the tail flat, and press a heaped tablespoon of Mushroom Stuffing over each tail. Sprinkle with Parmesan cheese. Set 3 inches below a broiler at high heat, and broil for 10 minutes.

# MUSHROOM-STUFFED BIRDS

**Preparation and cooking time: 1 1/2 hours**          **Serves 4–6**

Stuffed birds (*paupiettes* in French) always cause a little flutter when they arrive at the table. The secret is the addition of the crushed garlic and the mustard in the final half-hour of cooking. The mustard must be a fine one. Take the trouble to find one of the two noted if you don't already have these, or something even better. What mustard can do for a sauce!

If your meat market doesn't offer skinned, boned chicken thighs, prepare your own. It's easy. First, remove the skin: Grasp the loosest end of the skin, pull on it gently, and with a sharp knife point, slice the membrane holding the skin to the meat. Grasp the bone end, and with the sharp side of the knife facing up, slide the point along the bone until it comes out the other end. Still holding the bone end, but with the sharp side of the knife facing the bone and pressed against it, use the point of the knife to free the meat from the bone. Leave as little on the bone as possible. With this dish, I serve tender green snap beans cooked with a hint of dill. Add chilled, crisped salad of escarole hearts in an oil-and-vinegar dressing. And hot biscuits to sop up the sauce!

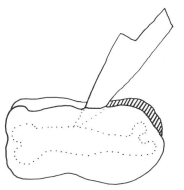

| | | | | |
|---|---|---|---|---|
| 4 | tablespoons butter | 4–6 | chicken thighs, skinned and boned |
| 2 | small onions, peeled | | |
| 1/2 | pound mushrooms, wiped | 2 | tablespoons butter |
| | Rind of 1/2 lemon | 2 | tablespoons all-purpose flour |
| 2 | tablespoons unflavored bread crumbs | 3/4 | cup chicken bouillon |
| 1/2 | cup minced parsley | 2 | large cloves garlic, peeled |
| 1 | teaspoon salt | 1 | tablespoon Maille or Pommery mustard |
| 1/4 | teaspoon black pepper | | Sprigs fresh parsley |
| 1/2 | teaspoon dried thyme | | |
| 1 | egg, slightly beaten | | |

Preheat the oven to 450° and place the rack in the top third. Put 2 tablespoons of the butter into a heavy enameled baking dish, and set it to melt in the oven. Withdraw the dish when the butter has melted.

In a large, heavy skillet over medium heat, melt the 2 remaining tablespoons of butter. In a food processor or by hand, mince the onions and mushrooms and stir them into the butter in the skillet. Stir and cook until the pan juices begin to dry up a little. Grate the lemon rind over the mixture and stir in the crumbs, parsley, salt, pepper, and thyme. Stir and cook until the parsley is wilted and looking darker, about another 3 minutes. Turn off the heat and stir in the beaten egg. When the egg has set, spread the boned thighs and fill each with a generous portion of the mushroom mixture. Secure with wooden toothpicks. Set the stuffed birds in the baking dish, then roll each bird over and return the dish to the oven. Bake, uncovered, for 30 minutes.

Melt the last 2 tablespoons of butter in the big skillet (don't clean it!) over low heat, and stir in the flour to make a smooth paste. Quickly beat the chicken bouillon into the paste and cook, stirring, until smooth and thick. Turn off the heat. When the chicken has baked for 20 minutes, remove from the oven, turn over each piece, and stir the cream sauce into the pan drippings—but don't pour it over the chicken pieces. Crush the garlic into the sauce, and stir in the mustard. Return to the oven and bake for another 30 minutes. Remove from the oven and stir the sauce into the caramelized drippings around the edge of the pan until these melt into the sauce. Garnish with a few sprigs of fresh parsley.

**Note**: The stuffing can be stretched to fill 8 thighs. Use 1 cup of bouillon and another 1/2 tablespoon of mustard.

**Variation: Mushroom-Stuffed Pork Chops**—Instead of chicken legs, buy thin, broad pork chops, 8 chops to serve 4 people (heartily). With a flat mallet, beat the pork meat to spread and thin it further (like scaloppine). Sprinkle a teaspoon of sage (preferably fresh, minced) over the chops, then prepare the stuffing as described. Divide the stuffing over 4 chops, and cover with 4 more chops. Season with salt and pepper, and bake as instructed for the chicken thighs with this difference: Make and pour the gravy over the chops before you put them in to bake. If the sauce dries, add a little more bouillon.

# CHICKEN CACCIATORE

**Preparation and cooking time: 1 1/4 hours**                    **Serves 6–8**

Chicken Cacciatore means "chicken, hunter style." Most often it is made with red wine and without onions, but we prefer it this way.

Use a whole chicken, cut up if economy is on your mind. Make it in a 12- to 14-inch chicken pan, a 12-inch electric fry pan, or cook on slow in an electric crock pot for 4 to 5 hours. Make it ahead—it keeps well. Olive oil gives it its distinctive flavor. Serve with plain pasta, white rice, or hot crusty Italian bread, and a tossed green salad. Strawberries and cream or stewed rhubarb makes a nice ending.

| | | | |
|---|---|---|---|
| 3 | pounds chicken thighs and legs | 2 | tablespoons minced fresh parsley |
| 1/4 | cup olive oil | 1 | tablespoon dried basil or 2 tablespoons minced fresh basil |
| 2 | medium-large onions, chopped | | |
| 2 | large cloves garlic, minced | 15 | ounces tomato sauce |
| 1/2 | cup dry white wine | 12 | ounces fresh mushrooms, sliced thick |
| 1 | teaspoon salt | | |
| 1/4 | teaspoon black pepper | | |

Separate thighs from legs and wipe the chicken.

Over high heat, sauté the parts in the oil until browned all over—10 to 15 minutes. Stir in the onions and cook 8 to 10 minutes more. Add the garlic and mix well. Add the wine, and after 2 minutes, scrape up the drippings that stick to the pan bottom. Sprinkle salt, pepper, and herbs over the chicken, stir a little, then pour on the tomato sauce and the mushrooms. Stir together, reduce the heat, cover, and cook for 15 minutes. Uncover and cook 15 minutes more, until the gravy is very thick.

When the oil looks as though it may begin to stand apart from the onion-mushroom substance of the sauce in an orange puddle, it is time to stop the cooking. If the oil separates, stir in a few tablespoons of bouillon or hot water to get a little moisture back into the dish.

# KIDNEYS 'N' CREAM

**Preparation and cooking time: 40 minutes**
**Soaking time: 4 hours or overnight**                    **Serves 4**

This is a rich creamy dish, wonderful over boiled rice. Serve with a lemony lettuce salad with lots of minced parsley on it. Veal kidneys are inexpensive and I prefer them in this to lamb kidneys, but lamb kidneys may be used. Crucial: Use fresh, fresh kidneys, soaked for several hours.

| | | | | |
|---|---|---|---|---|
| 1 | pound veal kidneys | 1/4 | teaspoon pepper |
| 1/2 | stick butter | 1/2 | teaspoon dried oregano |
| 1 | medium-large Bermuda onion, chopped | 1 | large clove garlic |
| 1 | large green pepper, chopped | 4 | ounces tomato sauce or puree |
| 8–10 | ounces mushrooms, stemmed and quartered | 1/8 | cup brandy |
| | | 1/2 | cup heavy cream |
| 1 | teaspoon salt | 4 | cups hot cooked rice |
| | | 1/2 | bunch parsley, minced fine |

Rinse the kidneys in cold water. With shears or a small, sharp knife, cut each knoblet of meat away from the core of fat and discard the cores. Rinse the kidney pieces in three changes of water, cover with cold water, and soak for at least 4 hours, or overnight, in the refrigerator.

Drain and dry the kidneys. In a large enameled or stainless-steel skillet (I use an electric skillet) over high heat, melt the butter and sauté the onion and pepper for 5 minutes. Add the mushrooms, salt, pepper, oregano, and mince the garlic into the mixture. Sauté for 5 minutes more. Add the kidneys, stir for a minute or so, then add the tomato sauce or puree. Sauté for 8 minutes more. Stir in the brandy and sauté for 2 minutes. Add the cream and sauté for 2 more minutes. Serve hot over rice, and offer parsley on the side.

# STEAK STROGANOFF

**Preparation and cooking time: 15–20 minutes**            **Serves 4**

"Chicken steak" is the name given in my part of the country to the little pieces of chuck that are tender as a boneless, more expensive cut, but have a nerve running down the center. Remove the nerve and presto! You have something almost as good as a real tenderloin cut, and great in this recipe.

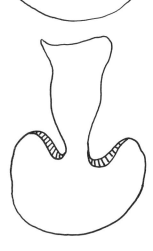

| | |
|---|---|
| 12 ounces mushrooms, wiped | 1/2 teaspoon Maille or |
| 6 tablespoons butter | Pommery mustard |
| Salt and pepper | 1/2 cup sour cream |
| 4 chicken steaks | 1 tablespoon minced parsley |
| 2 large garlic cloves | |

Cut off the tough ends of the mushroom stems. In a large, heavy skillet over medium-high heat, melt 4 tablespoons of the butter.

Slice the mushrooms 1/4 inch thick into the skillet, and shake the skillet and stir the mushrooms for 5 or 6 minutes or until the moisture has dried. Lightly salt and pepper the mushrooms, and scrape them into a serving plate. Set it in a warming oven on low.

With a small sharp knife, cut the tough nerve from the center of each steak and discard it. Salt and pepper the steak lightly. Crush the garlic and scrape a little over each piece of meat.

Melt the remaining butter in the skillet on high heat. When it froths, slide the steaks into the pan. Shake the pan for about 1 minute, or until the steaks are browned on one side, then at once turn the steaks. Shake and slide them around for another minute. Remove the pan from the heat. Arrange the mushrooms over the steaks. Still off heat, mash the mustard into the fat in the pan, scraping up the drippings congealed on the bottom, then return to the heat. Reduce the heat and stir the sour cream into the pan drippings. Do not boil—just barely heat through, scraping up the pan drippings. Scrape over the steaks and mushrooms, and serve at once garnished with minced parsley.

# MEAT LOAF STUFFED WITH MUSHROOMS

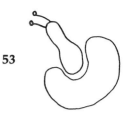

**Preparation and baking time: 50 minutes**     **Serves 4**

Good enough for company—but the mustard must be a very good one.

| | |
|---|---|
| 1 slice white bread | 1 teaspoon grated lemon rind |
| 1/2 cup milk | |
| 1 pound ground round | 2 tablespoons bread crumbs |
| 1 small onion | 1 cup bottled clam juice or beef bouillon |
| 1 teaspoon salt | |
| 1/8 teaspoon pepper | 2 tablespoons Pommery or Maille mustard |
| 3 tablespoons butter | |
| 12 ounces mushrooms, wiped | 1/4 teaspoon dried thyme |
| 3 large garlic cloves | Salt and pepper |
| 1/4 cup minced parsley | Parsley sprigs |

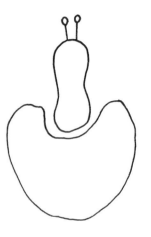

Preheat the oven to 450°.

Soak the bread in the milk, then beat the meat into it. Grate the onion and add it to the mixture, and mix in the salt and pepper. In a large baking dish, make half the meat mixture into a flat loaf. In a big skillet over medium heat, melt 2 tablespoons of the butter. Slice half the mushrooms 1/8 inch thick, and sauté until the moisture dries—5 or 6 minutes. Transfer the mushrooms to the loaf of meat and cover with the remaining meat. Set 4 stemmed mushroom caps stuffed with the remaining 1 tablespoon of butter on top of the loaf, and bake for 20 minutes.

Turn the heat to medium under the mushroom skillet. Mince the remaining mushrooms and sauté them in the skillet for 5 minutes. Crush the garlic, add to the skillet, stir in the parsley, rind, and bread crumbs, then the juice or bouillon, mustard, and thyme. Add salt and pepper to taste. Remove the baking dish from the oven, scrape the sauce in around the loaf, and bake for 20 minutes more. Turn the caps right side up and serve the meat loaf garnished with parsley.

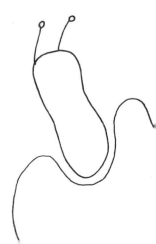

# LEG OF LAMB CHOPS

**Preparation time: 30 minutes**
**Baking time: 1 1/2 hours**                                    **Serves 4–8**

Leg of lamb sirloin chops are reasonably priced, irregular, bone-in chops from the upper portions of the leg. The meat is very flavorful, as the meat in bony cuts often is. Sautéed to bring out the flavor, then baked with mushrooms, they make a delicious casserole that is nifty with pasta and even better with lima beans (butter them with the fat this recipe tells you to discard), and a salad of escarole in a garlic dressing. Offer French bread: the gravy deserves attention! Though there is not a lot of meat here, the dish is very rich, and a small chop usually is enough for one.

| | | | |
|---|---|---|---|
| 4–8 | leg of lamb sirloin chops (2–3 pounds) | 12 | ounces mushrooms |
| 1/2 | cup all-purpose flour | 1/2 | cup dry white wine |
| | Salt and pepper | 1/2–1 | cup bottled clam juice or chicken bouillon |
| 2 | large garlic cloves, crushed | 1 | teaspoon dried or 2 teaspoons fresh chopped basil |
| 1 | medium Bermuda onion, coarsely chopped | 1/2 | cup heavy cream |

Preheat the oven to 375°.

Cut the nuggets of fat from the chops and put the fat into a large heavy skillet over medium heat to melt. Scatter the flour on a large plate. Salt and pepper the chops to your taste, and thoroughly flour them all over. When the fat is hot, put the chops into the skillet and cook them on each side until thoroughly browned—about 15 minutes. Shake the pan often. After you have turned each chop, sprinkle a little garlic over it. With tongs, lift the chops and place them in a baking dish that has a cover. Add the onion to the skillet, and sauté for 5 minutes.

Wipe the mushrooms and remove the tough ends of the stems. Slice them in T shapes about 1/4 inch thick, and distribute them over the onions. Cook the mushrooms with the onions for 5 minutes more. Pour the wine into the pan, and with a spatula, scrape up the congealed pan juices. Pour a half cup of the clam juice or bouillon into the pan, and stir and scrape for a minute or so, then pour over the chops. Sprinkle the basil over the chops, and cover the baking dish. Bake for 1 1/2 hours. Check toward the end, and if the sauce has dried considerably, add clam juice or bouillon.

When the cooking is complete, pour the sauce into a heat-proof cup or a gravy pitcher. Remove the fat and discard. Stir the cream into the remaining gravy and pour it back into the baking dish. Pour over the chops and mushrooms, and serve at once.

**Variations: Veal Shank Casserole**—Four pieces of veal shank 1 inch thick are wonderful cooked as described for the lamb sirloin chops. But flavor the veal with rosemary, preferably fresh rosemary, rather than with basil.
**Chuck Steak Casserole**—Like the bony cuts of veal and lamb, chuck steaks benefit from the mushroom treatment above. Flavor the steak with 2 or 3 tablespoons of good blue cheese, and omit the basil.
**Pork Chop Casserole**—Handle 4 one-inch-thick pork chops as described for Leg of Lamb Chops, but season with fresh thyme and/or sage instead of basil.

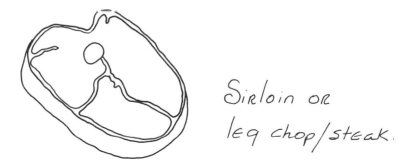

Sirloin or leg chop/steak.

# SCALLOPS AND MUSHROOMS IN CREAM

**Preparation and cooking time: 15 minutes**          **Serves 4**

Have you tried basil and orange yet?—ummmmm! The scallops must be fresh. Buy them from a reliable market a few hours before cooking.

| | |
|---|---|
| 1 | stick butter |
| 1 | pound medium mushrooms, stemmed |
| 2 | large garlic cloves |
| 4 | green onions, trimmed |
| 1/4 | teaspoon salt |
| | Pinch of pepper |
| 1/2 | cup dry white wine |
| 1/2–2/3 | pint heavy cream |
| 2 | tablespoons fresh-grated Parmesan cheese |

| | |
|---|---|
| 3/4 | pound bay scallops |
| 1 | teaspoon minced thyme |
| 1 | tablespoon grated orange rind |
| 1 | tablespoon minced basil |
| 1/2 | teaspoon salt |
| 1/4 | teaspoon pepper |
| 2 | thin orange slices, rind on, halved |
| 4 | small basil sprigs |

In a large, heavy skillet over medium heat, melt half the butter. Slice the mushrooms 1/4 inch thick into the butter. Mince the garlic and the onions over the mushrooms, then sauté until the moisture begins to dry up—5 or 6 minutes. Season the mushrooms with salt and pepper. Stir in the wine, and stir and cook until the wine has mostly evaporated. Stir in the 1/2 pint of cream, then the cheese, and cook until the sauce has thickened. Turn off the heat. Scrape into a serving dish.

When you are ready to serve, melt the remaining half of the butter in the same skillet over medium heat, and as soon as it is frothing, stir in the scallops and scrape up the pan juices. At once add the thyme, orange rind, basil, salt and pepper, and sauté the scallops for 1 more minute, or until they have just turned opaque. With a slotted spoon, scoop them into the mushroom sauce. Continue to simmer the sauce the scallops cooked in until it is reduced and thickened, then stir it into the scallop-mushroom mixture. If you wish a thinner sauce, stir in a little more cream. Garnish with orange slices and basil sprigs, and serve at once.

# COD STEAKS IN MUSHROOM SAUCE

**Preparation and baking time: 15 minutes**          **Serves 4**

The delicate flavor of cod is wonderful with this rich mushroom sauce.

| | | | |
|---|---|---|---|
| 4 | small cod steaks (1–2 pounds) Oil Salt and pepper | 1 | teaspoon minced basil or parsley |
| | | 1 | recipe Mushroom Sauce (below) |

Heat a broiler or an outdoor grill to high. Oil, salt, and pepper each side of the cod steaks, and mash a little minced herb over the top. Enclose in squares of heavy-duty aluminum foil, and broil or grill for 15 minutes or until the fish flakes through. Meanwhile, prepare the Mushroom Sauce. Lift from the foil to a serving platter and offer mushroom sauce.

## MUSHROOM SAUCE

**Preparation time: 15 minutes**          **Serves 4 to 6**

| | | | |
|---|---|---|---|
| 1/2 | pound mushrooms, wiped | 1/2 | teaspoon salt |
| 3 | tablespoons butter | 1/4 | teaspoon black pepper |
| 2 | large garlic cloves, crushed | 1 | teaspoon soy sauce |
| 1 | tablespoon all-purpose flour | 3/4–1 | cup heavy cream |

Mince the mushrooms in a food processor or chop them by hand. In a large saucepan over medium-high heat, sauté the mushrooms in the butter for 3 to 4 minutes. Crush the garlic over the mushrooms and cook 2 minutes more. Reduce the heat to low and stir in the flour, salt, pepper, and soy sauce; cook for 2 to 3 minutes. Add the cream all at once, and stir and cook until the sauce is smooth and thick—another 4 or 5 minutes. Don't cook it longer, as it will thicken from the heat of the saucepan.

# EXOTICS AND WILD MUSHROOMS

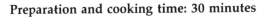

## CHINESE MUSHROOMS IN SHRIMP SAUCE

**Preparation and cooking time: 30 minutes**                    **Serves 4**

Dried mushrooms from Europe, particularly Italy, and from China and Japan, are wonderful for use in special dishes. To reconstitute them, soak them in tepid water to cover for about 20 minutes, then rinse them repeatedly under running water to remove the sand and grit often hidden in the gills. The consistency will be slithery, and the flavor stronger than in fresh mushrooms. Dried Chinese mushrooms look like open umbrellas with gnarly stems, rather similar to elegant cèpes, which are discussed on pages 62 and 63. The recipe below is fast-moving, so have everything ready before you begin.

| | | | |
|---|---|---|---|
| 3 | tablespoons corn oil | 2 | tablespoons soy sauce |
| 1 | teaspoon salt | 1 | tablespoon oyster sauce |
| 2 | large garlic cloves, minced | 2 | tablespoons dry sherry |
| 8 | dried Chinese mushrooms | 2 | large slices ginger, 1/4 |
| 8 | ounces mushrooms, wiped and sliced 1/8 inch thick | | inch thick, minced |
| | | 1 | tablespoon cornstarch |
| 3/4 | cup shredded Chinese cabbage | 1 | cup chicken broth or bottled clam juice |
| 1/2 | cup bamboo shoots, drained | 2 | teaspoons sugar |
| 8 | ounces raw shrimp, shelled and deveined | 4 | cups boiled white rice |

Soak the dried mushrooms in tepid water to cover. Dilute the cornstarch in the broth or clam juice. Line the ingredients up near the stove in the order in which the recipe lists them.

Get a wok or an electric skillet hot enough to skid a drop of water across its surface. Swirl in the oil. Spread the salt over it. Add the garlic, and stir-fry for 1 minute. Squeeze the water from the Chinese mushrooms and add them to the garlic. Add the mushroom slices and stir-fry for 3 minutes. Add the cabbage; stir-fry for 1 minute. Add the bamboo shoots; stir-fry 1 minute more. Add the shrimp; stir-fry for 1 minute.

Season with soy sauce, oyster sauce, sherry, and ginger, stirring constantly. Pour the broth or clam juice into the wok, and stir and toss the ingredients while cooking for 1 minute more, or until the sauce has thickened. Sprinkle with sugar, and taste. Add more soy sauce if desired. Serve at once with boiled rice, and offer soy sauce on the side.

## CELERY, MUSHROOMS, AND FLOWERS

**Preparation and cooking time: 15 minutes**                    **Serves 4**

Roll-cut the celery for this: Place a stalk in front of you, place a carving knife at a diagonal, cut the stalk through, roll over to the other side and cut again. This makes a nifty vegetable dish with grilled meats and chicken. Daylilies and squash blossoms are edible fresh flowers. The lilies are sold by many greengrocers.

|   |   |   |   |
|---|---|---|---|
| 2 | tablespoons corn oil | 1 | small heart celery |
| 8 | ounces mushrooms, wiped | 1/2 | cup canned water chestnuts, drained |
| 1 | tablespoon soy sauce |  |  |
| 1/2 | teaspoon salt | 4 | yellow daylily or squash blossoms |
| 1 | teaspoon sugar |  |  |

Measure the oil. Cut the tough ends from the mushrooms and cut the mushrooms into T shapes, 1/4 inch thick. Measure the soy sauce, salt, sugar. Cut the ends from the celery, separate the stalks, rinse them, and roll cut.

Get a wok or an electric skillet hot enough to skid a drop of water across its surface. Swirl in the oil. Add all the mushroom slices and stir-fry for 2 minutes. Sprinkle with soy, salt, and sugar; add the celery chunks; and stir and fry 3 to 4 minutes more or until the celery just begins to lose its bright green color. Add a little more soy, if desired, stir in the water chestnuts, and scrape onto a serving plate and garnish with flowers. Serve at once.

# MONGOLIAN HOT POT

**Preparation time: 30–40 minutes**                    **Serves 4–6**

A simple way to let friends cook their own dinner around a Mongolian hot pot, a heated fondue pot, or an electric saucepan or skillet. Freeze the meat slightly so it's firm enough to cut sliver thin. I serve this with a big loaf of peasant bread, butter, a green salad, and cheese. Cellophane noodles are sold in oriental and gourmet shops.

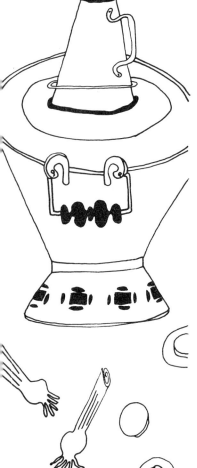

| | |
|---|---|
| 2 ounces cellophane noodles | 1/2 small Chinese cabbage |
| Hot water | 4 cups boiling water |
| 6 cups chicken broth | 1 bunch enoki or snow puff |
| 3 scallions, trimmed | mushrooms |
| 1 large garlic clove | 1/2 cup soy sauce |
| 1/2-inch piece fresh | 1/2 tablespoon brown sugar |
| ginger root, sliced | dissolved in 2 tablespoons |
| 1/4 bunch parsley | water |
| 2 pounds boneless lamb | 1 tablespoon dry sherry |
| from the leg | 1 tablespoon sesame oil |
| 8 ounces 3- to 4-inch mush- | 1 tablespoon peanut butter |
| rooms | dissolved in 2 tablespoons |
| 1/2 pound spinach, washed | boiling water |

Cover the cellophane noodles with hot water and soak 30 minutes. Drain. Meanwhile, heat the broth to boiling. Trim the scallions down to the white and in a food processor, a blender, or by hand, mince with the garlic, sliced ginger root, and parsley. Add to the broth and turn off the heat.

With a very sharp knife, cut the lamb into slices 1/8 inch thick by 2 by 3 inches or so and place them decoratively on four to six shallow soup plates. Wipe the mushrooms and remove the tough ends of the stems. Slice them in T shapes 1/8 inch thick and arrange with the lamb. Put 2 spinach leaves on each plate; arrange the remainder on a large platter. Pull the cabbage leaves apart and cut the ribs free. Cut each rib into sticks and blanch them in the boiling water for 3 minutes; then turn off the heat.

Trim a third off the bottoms of the enoki mushrooms, break into groups, and place with the spinach, ribs, and drained noodles cut in half on the platter.

In a Chinese soup bowl or a similar container, combine the soy sauce, brown sugar dissolved in water, sherry, sesame oil, and peanut butter dissolved in water. Pour a tablespoonful or two into each of four to six small sauce bowls (such as are used for butter for artichokes).

Bring the broth back to a boil, transfer to the serving container, set in the center of the table, and keep it simmering. Put the platter in the center of the table and place a soup plate and chopsticks before each guest so he or she can cook his or her own meat and mushrooms in the broth. When the meat and mushrooms have been eaten, pour the contents of the platter into the broth, cook 3 to 5 minutes, and serve as soup.

## MUSHROOMS, SPINACH, AND CHESTNUTS

**Preparation and cooking time: 10 minutes**               **Serves 4**

Stir-frying is one of the best ways to cook vegetables. This combination is great with American-style meats and chicken.

| | | | |
|---|---|---|---|
| 3 | tablespoons corn oil | 1 | teaspoon sugar |
| 2 | large cloves garlic | | Soy sauce |
| 8 | ounces mushrooms, wiped | 1/2 | cup drained, sliced water |
| 1/2 | teaspoon salt | | chestnuts |
| 1 | pound spinach, washed | | |

Measure the oil, and peel the garlic. Remove the tough ends of the mushrooms and cut into T shapes 1/8 inch thick. Measure the sugar, and place all the ingredients in the order listed by the stove.

Get a wok or an electric skillet hot enough to skid a drop of water across its surface. Swirl in the oil and crush the garlic into it. Cook, shaking the pan, until it browns. Add all the mushroom slices, and stir-fry them until the moisture dries—5 to 6 minutes. Sprinkle with salt. Stir in the spinach and stir-fry until it wilts. Turn off the heat. Season with sugar and soy sauce to taste and mix in water chestnut slices. Serve at once.

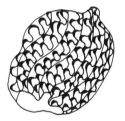

# WILD MUSHROOMS AND WILD RICE

**Preparation and cooking time: 1 hour**                    Serves 4–6

The wild mushrooms illustrated here, cèpes and morels, are two of the costly dried imports sold by gourmet shops at $7 and $13 an *ounce*. The little dunce caps have an extraordinary pungency. Both types are reconstituted by soaking in hot water for 30 minutes. Rinse away all sand and grit before using the mushrooms and strain the soaking water if you plan to include it in the dish. Fresh cèpes are a real prize. They turn up now and then at under $5 a half pound. They are heaven with wild rice, as here. Fresh wild mushrooms are handled in the same manner as cultivated mushrooms—the tough tip ends are cut away and the caps cleaned, preferably without a lot of washing in water. Just wipe them clean. Wild mushrooms and wild rice make an elegant side dish for duck, goose, lamb, liver. Shiitake mushrooms have the flavor of fresh cèpes and may be used as a substitute, but cook these only a minute or two.

|   |   |   |   |
|---|---|---|---|
| 4 | ounces wild rice | 1 | teaspoon grated lemon rind |
| 2 1/4–1/2 | cups water | | Pinch of salt and pepper |
| 1/2 | teaspoon salt | 2 | tablespoons finely minced parsley |
| 4 | tablespoons butter | | |
| 1/4 | cup thin carrot rounds | 1 | round orange, peel on |
| 1 | small clove garlic | | |
| 1/2 | pound fresh cèpes | | |

Wash the rice in cold water. Over high heat in a small, heavy saucepan covered with a tightly fitting lid, bring to a rapid boil 2 1/4 cups of the water, the rice, salt, and 1 tablespoon of the butter. Reduce the heat to very low, stir the rice once, cover and cook 45 minutes. Add 1/4 cup more water if all the water is gone and stir in the carrot rounds. Cover and continue to cook until the rice is perfectly tender, about 10 minutes more. Turn off the heat.

While the carrots are cooking, set the remaining butter to melt in a heavy skillet over medium heat. Mince the garlic into it and, one at a time, cut the tough stem ends from the mushrooms and slice the caps into 1/4-inch-thick T shapes into the butter. Stir and cook 4 or 5 minutes until the pieces begin to look shriveled. Stir in the lemon rind. Season with salt, pepper and parsley, stir 1 minute more and turn off the heat. Toss with the rice gently so as not to break the carrot rounds. Scrape into a serving dish, garnish with the orange round, and serve hot.

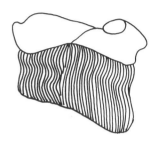

**Variations: Fresh Cèpes Provençale**—Three or 4 large cèpes will serve one person as an appetizer or first course. Rinse, drain, and stem the mushrooms; reserve the stems. Season with salt and pepper, and sauté the caps in 3 tablespoons of good olive oil for 5 or 6 minutes. Chop the stems with 1 large garlic clove, and stir into the cèpes with 1 tablespoon unflavored bread crumbs. Turn off the heat and stir in 2 tablespoons minced parsley and 2 teaspoons lemon juice. Taste, and increase the seasonings if desired. Serve on hot, buttered toast.

**Shiitake Mushrooms, Fresh**—These are cultivated mushrooms, but resemble the fresh cèpes in flavor, and may be used as a substitute where fresh cèpes are called for. Cook only a minute or two, or they will toughen. Delicious!

**Creamed Morels Escoffier**—Dried morels may be prepared as cèpes, above, though for my taste, they are almost too rich in flavor. Dry the little caps after they have been reconstituted in hot water and pick them through carefully with your fingers. I have found bits of black cinder in them on occasion, and it doesn't taste good.

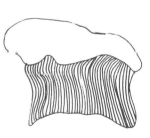

**Fresh Morels Provençale**—Prepare the stemmed and quartered or halved morels as described for Fresh Cèpes Provençale, but cook them for 10 to 12 minutes, and use the juice of 1 whole lemon per pound of caps.

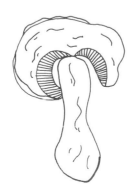

# RECIPE LIST/INDEX